WHITE ROAD OF THORNS

WHITE ROAD OF THORNS

Journalist's Diary – Trials and Tribulations of the Japanese American Internment During World War II

MARY Y NAKAMURA

Library of Congress Control Number: 2015912556
ISBN: Hardcover   978-1-5035-9214-8
                   Softcover   978-1-5035-9213-1
                   eBook   978-1-5035-9212-4

Print information available on the last page.

Rev. date: 08/17/2015

To order additional copies of this book, contact:
Xlibris
1-888-795-4274
www.Xlibris.com
Orders@Xlibris.com
716530

CONTENTS

To my late parents, Tokumon and Hisa Aoki, with love and gratitude.
To my late siblings, Grace Nakashima (younger
sister) and Roy Aoki and Frank Aoki (elder brothers),
with love and fond childhood memories.
To Eddie, the love of my life for over sixty-
five years, with happiness and trust.
To Rod, Nora, Tom, Daniel, and Kristin, with love and
happiness, making life exciting and interesting.

Hisa Aoki, 1939

Photo was taken in Los Angeles, CA when she published
her first book "Kokoro no Kage" (Shadow of the Heart)

Aoki Wedding Tokyo, Japan, 1925

Aoki Family, Oakland, CA, 1932

WHITE ROAD OF THORNS
Translator's Comments

This book is a diary of Yamamoto Asako (pen name of Aoki Hisa) from the time of the outbreak of the war between the United States and Japan, her confinement at Santa Anita, and her time at Gila Relocation Center until her selection as a passenger on the *Gripsholm* for the second wartime exchange of nationals between the United States and Japan. She was living in Los Angeles when World War II broke out.

A word on the meaning of the title: *A road of thorns* is an expression used to express experiencing hardship and suffering. White Road is the path of the orbit of the moon. The sun's path is referred to as Yellow Road. The author is alluding to a trying period in her journey of life. Translator's comments are in parenthesis with asterisk. Names may not be correct because of variant readings in Japanese. Translation is made as close to the writer's script as possible to convey the writer's feelings. This results in a degree of awkwardness because of the differences in sentence structure of the two languages, but it serves to more closely identify with the author. Where a word or terminology is not clear, a translator note is added to provide clarification. A word of explanation about the Spanish Consulate's involvement with the Japanese community. During World War II, Spain represented Japan's interest in the United States, and Switzerland represented the United States in Japan.

This is probably the only detailed written account of that period recorded as events unfolded. From that alone, this is an important historical document. Others might have kept diaries but not in such detail. While there have been many writings of the Japanese internment, none are as vividly descriptive and in such detail as this account. Recollections written years after the fact would necessarily be abbreviated without details of day-by-day events. Those who were teenagers at that time weren't affected nearly as much by the emotional and especially the economic impact evacuation had on adults, so their recollections may be centered more on social and recreational events, giving a totally different perspective on the internment.

For those who spent time in Santa Anita and Gila, this is a must read; and even for those who were interned elsewhere, this will stir memories of their own experiences. For the younger generation who are more concerned with constitutional issues, and rightly so, this diary will offer a glimpse into the emotional impact of internment on two generations of the Japanese community and what they went through.

While the writer was a first-generation Japanese national and all who lived through those trying times may not have harbored the same sentiments, the experience itself or something similar was one shared by almost all persons of Japanese ancestry living in the United States at that time.

This translation is the property of Mary Y. Nakamura and may not be used for any purpose without her authorization. This book was published in 1953 in Tokyo, Japan. Translated April 2015, Harbor City, California. Translator: Archie Miyamoto.

WHITE ROAD OF THORNS
Living in Wartime America
Yamamoto Asako

Foreword 1

In this modern age when human traffic is developed, in every country, many foreigners reside there with that being the base for their livelihood; and while they connect their life to that country and grasp one strand of the net that constitutes the life of that country and contributes to the cultural development of that country, once war breaks out, for those who live in that country and are citizens of the country, that is now the enemy, without knowing anything, suddenly labeled "enemies," and the foundation of their livelihood built there is taken away, or they are purged from that country and, truly as the word says, are thrown on the streets. If one dies on the battlefield, he may be honored; but having survived and having your means of livelihood taken away and no one to say, "You are an honorable casualty," they are the unfortunate ones.

Mrs. Aoki (Yamamoto Asako is Aoki Hisa's pen name) is one of the people who met that fate. For her, who with her husband, went to America to work at educating, lived there for twenty years, had completely accepted America, and was even intending to be buried there, it was a war without pity. It goes without saying, with many Japanese, it became necessary to spend a camp life and in the end abandoned the place she meant to be buried and had to return to Japan. She was a talented writer, and among Japanese community, she was known by her pen name of Yamamoto Asako, so she wrote down the daily history of this unforeseen fate, centered on event around her, in detail in a diary and put that into print is this book.

And she did this work of leaving a valuable document without being conscious of what she was doing. Nothing other than what she heard directly and what she saw and what she thought is written, so that is all; and in each word and each phrase, there is no falsehood and no pretense, and it can be said what those others who shared the same fate "heard with their ears, saw with their eyes and what they thought" are passed on through her and quietly relayed. There is resentment, there is hate, and there is also excitement but not of those that are exceptionally high or low but those of everyone, and that is just honestly portrayed.

Writing that is not driven by intent to create literature but a record of what was heard, what was seen, and what was felt is, on the contrary, of more interest than pure literature. It is because its essence is not exceptional literary genius but the feelings of an ordinary human being.

I have never written a preface to something written by someone else, but I was asked by an old friend, Ando Masazumi, who, this year now, I have known for half a century and read the proof of this book. I have also met Mrs. Aoki, and it came to be that I decided to write this preface.

May 1952, Kamakura Mountain Villa, Japan
Hasegawa Korekiyo

WHITE ROAD OF THORNS

Foreword 2

On this occasion, Ms. Yamamoto Asako has published her experiences living in America during the war, *White Road of Thorns*. I believe it was a very timely decision.

The proof arrived by air mail. I avidly read as if sucked in by it. It is truly Ms. Yamamoto's writing. While just ordinary writing of a diary, each and every bit gets to the core. It has truthfulness. Also, points which men would overlook are clearly recorded. It is not like a popular novel. It is a pure record. It is experience without falsehood. This is wherein the value of this book lies.

The events of the day her husband was taken by the FBI, her arrival at the horse stables in Santa Anita, when one reads those, without being aware of, tears flow.

In the hidden side of war, what is not generally known, there are many tragedies like this! One example of this is what this has taught me. It is an eternal commemoration.

Once it passes the throat, one forgets the heat. This is human nature. Our countrymen in America too nowadays have completely forgotten about what happened in wartime. To forget is certainly good in one aspect. Now that the war is over, there is nothing better than to forget the unpleasant! Some say that. However, because we easily forget, soon, we repeat the same thing.

From that meaning, the record of sad events during the war absolutely must be left for those who come later. This is necessary for the happiness of mankind.

There is no crime worse than war. There is no tragedy as bad as war. In its hidden side, there are many hidden tragedies. There are countless sad casualties. We must not forget this. And we must not repeat this tragedy lightly.

As long as we have nation states, it is natural to have war! There are people who casually say this. However, even if we have nation states, there is no reason to bite each other like wild beasts. The cause of war is arrogance and greed that lies in the breast of people. Therefore, if only people's thinking is purified, no matter how many countries there are, they should be able to live in friendship. This is the point on which mankind must reflect.

Rearmament is all right. There are occasions when war cannot be avoided. Think about this. Even if war cannot be avoided, to women and children who know nothing, we must not let them repeat this kind of tragedy. Also, we must not let these sad events happen to people of other countries!

If this kind of thinking is present in the leaders and the military of all countries, it is fine. If not, the suffering of mankind cannot be measured.

Mistreatment of prisoners of war. Punishment of war criminals. Treatment of wounded soldiers.

Against these too, with this feeling at all costs, proper measure should be taken. When thinking about such matters, more than anyone, I want leaders and military men to read this book.

In any event, I rejoice that this book was published. At the same time, to the effort and undertaking, my heartfelt respect.

1952, late June, under a blazing sun, Denver, Colorado
Tamai Yoshitaka

I. THIS ADVERSITY: PENANCE
FOR SINS IN A PRIOR LIFE?

December 7, 1941
(Japan Time: December 8, Sixteenth Year of Showa)

A bolt out of the blue sky, like water in a one's sleeping ear, unimaginably fearful, cruel this reality—indescribable waves of strong shock and fear over my entire body; if I try to stop it, it becomes even stronger and overcomes me!

"At present, Japanese airplanes are bombing Hawaii's Pearl Harbor!"

I heard those words from a young waiter at the Chinese restaurant, Sankohro, in Los Angeles. Unimaginable that it was winter; it was a warm Sunday, around eleven o'clock, a church friend from Oakland, Mrs. Michinoue, said, "Let me stay with you today and leisurely listen to Buddhist stories."

It had been a while since she had last visited, and we decided to have a Chinese lunch, and our family had taken her to the Sankohro. Before the food had been served, we heard this kind of news, and it was unexpected like a pole out of a bush, and I thought, *Not really—it must be some kind of mistake!*

And with a feeling of not accepting it right away, we all looked at each other as if fooled by a fox.

Had it been June or July when the direction of clouds in U.S. and Japan relations were very bad, war was not unthinkable, but now negotiations were ongoing with Ambassador Kurusu, and the feeling that this could not be true was stronger.

"Somehow it seems to be true," the restaurant owner, Mr. Kida, came out and said. He was always relaxed and calm but now was pale and coughing a bit. My chest is pounding! The waves from the stone of uncertainty that had been thrown into my chest, while half believing, gets bigger. Ordinarily delicious dishes of food are all bitter and tasteless. I taste strange saliva in my mouth.

My two daughters, Yoko, age twelve, and Sachiko, age ten, ate so fast it was difficult to see where they swallowed it and hurriedly went out to buy a special edition of newspapers being announced on sale in the street.

Looking at the newspaper they brought back, in large bold letters that appeared two inches square, "WAR . . .," I involuntarily gasped! I had been completely mentally unprepared and felt as though I had been hit with a sledge hammer. Blood rushed to my face, and breathing became difficult, and in inverse proportion, my feet inside my shoes, starting from the toes, started to get cold as ice. I looked down, covering both cheeks, and tried to organize my confused mind. My husband, with a sunken voice, said, "This is something we cannot do anything about, so let us all remain calm and do our best."

Mrs. Michinoue said, "Tomorrow tomorrow's wind will blow. Let us go with whatever happens."

Our two daughters, after the meal was over, had been promised an interesting movie, but these young children seemed to have understood what kind of situation they had been placed in. And said, "This is no time to see a movie. Let's hurry up and go home."

On the way home, Japanese we met all had worried faces drained of blood. What should we do? Dragged around by upsetting emotions, the afternoon hours passed.

After dinner at seven thirty, we turned on the switch to the shortwave radio and listened to news from Japan. As if it was time to match the tempo, the Imperial Rescript on the war and General Tojo's speech came in.

"Ah, ah, war had really started. But why did Japan launch a surprise attack?"

Cold sweat broke out on my face; in front of my eyes, I saw endless ash-colored waves. In those waves, which probably continue on to a pitch-dark land of Miyo (Buddhist term for nether world), floating and sinking, writhing, writhing in agony, I saw our family. My mind, which had reached saturation point with surprise, suffering, and sadness, was numb, and I could not think clearly. My husband gloomily says, "We may be chased on to a road of thorns with our lives at stake, but we have no choice but to do our best each time."

December 8

Must be because I was excited, I awoke while it was still faintly dark. The children, when it came time to go to school, seemed somewhat hesitant, which was understandable.

Mrs. Michinoue who stayed over last night appeared as though she did not get a good sleep after all and had heavy eyelids, but she said, "Under these circumstances, please be careful." And she went home.

After 10:00 a.m., from Shimano Sensei's (teacher's) wife, there was a phone call informing us Sensei was taken in by the FBI at eleven last night. By around noon, we learned many had been taken into custody from last night to this morning. All were acquaintances. Among them were those attending a wedding reception or attending a farewell party for someone who was to return to Japan shortly or attending a victory celebration over Japanese victories. When it came to taking into custody members of the veteran's association and officials of the navy association, very strict cautionary measures were taken, and it seems women were among them. Those people were sent to country jails or confined at the immigration center. Stories were relayed that officials of the various organizations knew that they could end up in that situation at any time and in preparation for being taken, had handbags with everyday necessities prepared.

Then how about us? We might be among those who should be prepared. My head is confused with uncertainty.

December 9

"Remember Pearl Harbor!" These signs were posted here and there on the streets. Even as I quietly cowered at home, the tragedies of families of those taken into custody continued to be relayed. Because the breadwinner of the family had been taken, they say there are some families grieving because of difficulties in livelihood. It is very sad to hear of a wife who became mentally unbalanced when her husband was taken into custody.

December 21

The wind blew during the night, and the slamming sound from one of the screen doors of the next room that had come loose woke me up. Thinking about this and that, about what was yet to come, tears flowed without end, and I ended up unable to sleep. I also heard the noise at 2:00 a.m., 3:00 a.m., and 4:00 a.m. About daylight, I fell into deep sleep; and when I awoke, it was close to eight. Since war broke out, Japanese school was closed; we were without jobs. It is a very dreary feeling.

The wind calmed down, and the sunshine is beautiful. I have heard through news on the winds that in Japan at that, moment, they are celebrating victories; but for us, there is no Christmas or New Years. Even then, those who were taken into custody at Terminal Island Confinement Center, county jails, Tujunga Camp, or those families sent to faraway camps in Arizona and Montana, those people must be much more lonely and suffering much more.

Today was a day with many visitors. By the time the sun went down, it was eleven persons, four who came during lunch hour; we had them eat whatever was available with our family. They were all those who had lost their jobs because of the war. We spent two or three hours looking at each other with worried faces with no plan of what we should do. Luckily, at my place, we have enough food to eat to last until June or July of next year. But the big problem is rent, and we have to figure out what to do about this.

December 22

The sun is warm, but the wind is cold. During morning hours, designed dress patterns, afternoon visited Uncle T's place. Uncle T is a Kibei Nisei (Nisei who lived for a time in Japan); his wife is a Nisei (Japanese American) raised in the United States, but she has a deep interest in Japanese-language education.

President Roosevelt, it is said, is presently considering the establishment of a wartime committee above the present cabinet. It seems like this supreme wartime committee will consist of three or five members, and they say it will be made up of Windell Willkie

(Republican presidential candidate, 1940), Adm. William D. Leahy (consul to French Vichy government), VP Henry A. Wallace, and Phillip Murray (president of Congress of Industrial Organization-CIO). Further, news sources say President Roosevelt is already thinking of preparing an important post for Mr. Willkie.

Today the Civil Defense Bureau and the Department of Agriculture announced that if the war appears to be prolonged, for the coming spring and summer farm labor, it would be natural to have women register in preparation for mobilization.

December 23

It is hail! It is cold to the core of one's soul. There is news all over the place that on the Pacific coast, there are about forty Japanese submarines rising and submerging. Can that be true?

A group of male and female correspondents who had returned from an observation tour of China and Japan are writing or going on lecture tours and intensely saying in a loud voice, "Do not underestimate the Japanese Navy!" But the attitude of the general public is, it's Japan that couldn't defeat Chiang Kai-shek in four years—and do not listen.

It says Prime Minister Churchill of England suddenly arrived in Washington today. They say it is to make plans for eliminating Hitlerism from all over the world.

December 24

Today morning hours were spent designing dress patterns. At this time, writing essays and children's stories have broken off from me. The only thing that is capable of connecting with my future is dressmaking. I have studied American dressmaking, Hawaiian dressmaking, and

Japanese dressmaking. I want to take the stylish parts and design a Far Eastern dress. Therefore, this is undoubtedly a problem that will require considerable effort and many years.

Two or three students came bringing tuition and gifts. Even then, what a lonely Christmas. My educational institute did not request donations. And as a result at year end, we would receive donations of rice and shoyu to last a year or year and a half; and usually with other gifts, one small room would be filled. Therefore, even though it is lonely this year, being able to look back at those years is a joyful thing. Even the two children, I believe having given them the memory of being able to look back at the times they received very nice gifts was a good thing.

Today we received one chicken, so knowing at least we will be able to have a Christmas dinner tomorrow, I put it in the ice box.

December 25

Cold. Because of smudge pots, the sky is dirty and gray from afternoon hail. It is a lonely Christmas as a citizen of enemy Japan. Every year in our living room, we would decorate a Christmas tree of about six feet, but this year is a pitiful-looking tree of less than three feet that Sachiko won in a class raffle at the public school. Under these circumstances, it is probably better not to celebrate Christmas or New Year for Japanese families. No! Even if they wanted to, most are probably unable to.

At my sister's place, all three members of the family have the flu, and young son Nobuhiro had convulsions twice; so from afternoon, he was hospitalized at Japanese hospital. I went to the nearby hospital twice, but it seems it isn't serious, and he will be discharged in two or three days. They say brother-in-law Yamamoto is resting at home, so I told Yoko to be careful many times and gave her medicine and lemon to take with her to her uncle's place seven miles away by street car.

It must have been three days after war broke out; when I got on a street car, a Mexican woman intentionally stepped on my left instep. She was a mean-looking, stocky women of about forty-five or forty-six with uneven white powder on her face. I kept silent and withdrew my foot. Rather than being vexed, I was sad. Tears moistened my eyes. White women and children were not concerned with the war and up to today were busy Christmas shopping. With wartime economy booming, factory workers are rolling in money. But after buying all you can buy and after this holiday season is over, how will it be? January is still fine. What about after February is past and March arrives? Tax time arrives. It seems wartime tax will be 225 percent more than peacetime and will be the equivalent to two-month pay of the average worker.

Today's radio said, "To everyone, as a big Christmas present, a U.S. Navy plane sank a Japanese submarine."

However, Japanese people said, "You say that, but sinking is a submarine's business," and do not believe it.

December 27

My husband, to discuss Japanese School Association matters from 10:00 a.m., went to the association meeting. Since it is a time when money for even office fees is not forthcoming, it was decided to move the Japanese School Association administrative office to my house. Since Association Director Nagashima Sensei was taken to the Montana Confinement Center, after that, all administrative matters became the responsibility of Sugimachi Sensei, Yoshizumi Sensei, Hoshimiya Sensei, and my husband, the four of them.

The two hundred twenty-plus Japanese schools in the United States finally were decided that they be indefinitely closed. We have to also decide on assistance for unemployed teachers. Their numbers, in Southern California alone, numbered about three hundred. However, unemployment assistance for the unemployed in San Pedro is even more urgent. There are an estimated ten thousand people who are in need of food for today and tomorrow. We have to help them as soon as possible. It seems that is a problem now facing the citizen's association.

Japanese Americans who are in the military service, it seems as of today, cannot be sent to war. It seems it is because authorities fear the consequences of even one who might go over to the enemy.

We are surprised at how carefully the FBI is investigating the living situation of the Japanese community. Veteran's (Japanese military veterans) Association, Japan Association, Prefecture Association, Japanese schools, instructors and texts, Shinto groups, and others covering everything.

In the text approved by Japan's Ministry of Education, they say the article that excited Americans the most was "One Day in Honolulu." "Honolulu is American territory, and the same words are used to see someone off to Yokohama." This meant, "The Japanese think Honolulu is an extension of Japan."

The Japanese text says, "The population of Hawaii is 380,000 of which 150,000 are Japanese, and they are engaged in agriculture, fishing industry, commerce, and all types of other activities."

The FBI interprets this as "Among the 150,000 are over 110,000 Japanese Americans. While America treats them as Americans, Japan considers them to be Japanese. It must be because they have dual citizenship. That is why they cannot be trusted."

Really, there is this way to look at it.

(Dual citizenship. Until 1924, children of a Japanese father were considered by Japan to be a Japanese citizen. Children born after that time had to be registered with the local Japanese consulate within two weeks or were barred from obtaining dual citizenship after that time The disadvantage of not being registered is they are non-Japanese and not the "legal" child of the father and thus unable to inherit their father's property in Japan. Another disadvantage of dual citizenship was you could be conscripted for military service if in Japan.)

December 28

When I did the laundry in the morning, around noon it started to rain. My younger sister's boy's temperature stabilized, and I was told he will be discharged from the hospital tomorrow.

A special edition of the Japanese-language newspaper came out saying Issei (first-generation Japanese) will turn in all shortwave radios and camera to the police by 11:00 p.m., Monday. It was in last night's English newspaper. The one at our house is a radio with both shortwave and normal listening, so we called the radio shop and had the short-wave portion removed.

Today and tomorrow are the busiest days for the radio shop, and they are having a busy time. However, it seems families with only Nisei are allowed to listen to shortwave. They say many Americans are listening to English broadcasts from Japan. They say Manila has fallen four days ago, but it will not be in the English newspapers until after about a week. It says in the attack on Manila, there were women soldiers in the Japanese Army, and they were shooting machine guns, so we killed them—can there be a reason for women soldiers? There must be some kind of mistake.

If rights and interests of Oceania is controlled by Japan; the first problem will be rubber, then tin; and because of that, they say new tires will probably be unavailable in the future. And it is written because raw silk will not be coming from Japan; by April, silk stockings will disappear and be replaced with nylon. For military purposes, silk is used for parachutes and wrapping artillery powder, and America will probably start using nylon. But you can't deny that is a substitute.

Sewing instructor Mrs. M dropped by. She said, "For twelve years, I sewed only American things, but in the end, Americans are Americans, and Japanese are Japanese. Since the war started, this Christmas, Americans ask me if everything is okay, but not one said Merry Christmas to me."

December 29

During the morning hours, it rained on and off, and even the clear part of the sky was fairly dark. Husband went to clear up the school association office. Our house radio was inspected by the local police and passed; the camera was put in police storage.

Since the outbreak of war, the activities of Reds (Communists) really stand out. Despicable Reds, subversive Communists, the ones who are the most harmful to the Japanese community are them. What reason do they have to harm those of us of the same blood? The scoundrels' newspaper, *Countrymen*, is published three times a week. It is a small paper in both English and Japanese and is actively distributed. And they seem to be making an effort to have it seen by as many as possible.

The ring leader is reportedly the son of a former reporter for the Japanese paper xxxx and said to be a Kibei (American citizen educated in Japan) who graduated or did not graduate from W University and said to have been affected with this thinking since he was in Japan. Using the fact that they have a print shop and sufficient funds, they are jumping around as if their time has come. They number in the tens and hundreds. You cannot hate them enough. The other day, the person walking around Japan town and sowing the rascal's paper, *Countrymen*, was a comely Japanese lady of about forty-five or forty-six. Before, I had written an essay entitled "The Red Mrs." The lady who came to force a sale of *Countrymen* on me was a very pretty young lady wearing a greenish brown one-piece dress. At that time, I said, "It is not that I don't want to part with 5¢. I don't want to dirty my eyes." And I sent her away. I pray we can remove this cause which creates confusion among our honest countrymen.

The Americans are making a lot of noise because they say the Japanese Military successively, heavily bombed the demilitarized city of Manila. At a press conference, Defense Secretary Hull severely criticized the bombing of a demilitarized city, and Representative Hoyler (sic) said, "To bomb Tokyo and Kobe, we had many bombers and bombs, but we gave them to others, and it is regrettable we cannot do this right away. But after waiting and when we can, we will burn up all the cities of Japan."

With victories to date, Japan is expected to get five hundred thousand tons of heavy oil. Meanwhile, the United States has not been able to get rubber, and they say great effort is being made to find a way to manufacture artificial rubber, but will that go smoothly?

Today I had a reason to visit Mr. K's home, but in the streetcar and on the street, I was subjected to continuous unfriendly looks.

December 30

It looks like rain. It is cold and damp. The Chinese are wearing on their chest a white button about an inch in size that has on it in red ink saying they are Chinese. Since war broke out, Chinese have been mistaken for Japanese and treated with contempt, so this is a way to avoid that and is typical of Chiang Kai-shek's people.

December 31

Sky is clear. It does not feel like the last day of the year at all. Even though I awoke, I did not feel like getting up and doing anything, so I laid in bed and thought of this and that for a long time.

At around 8:00 a.m., my sister phoned and said, "Today I received a lot of *mochi* (rice cakes), so I will bring *mochi* for offerings and eating." So I decided not to go to Japanese town to buy *mochi*. Afternoon, Mr. I and my sister brought *mochi*, so we had enough.

Becoming an enemy national with a pitch-dark future, I didn't think it was a time to be celebrating New Year, but I decided to at least make a semblance of a feast. Chicken, bamboo shoots, sweet boiled taro, daikon (Japanese radish), julienne, *kimpira gobo* (a string-cut burdock dish), black beans, etc. Herring roe is not coming from Japan and is not on sale in town, and fresh *kamaboko* (fish paste sausage) is not available because fish is not available, so I used canned ones.

I cleaned the house with the children, but a large house like this takes about this much time every day for a week to get it cleaned.

On the thirtieth, President Roosevelt announced that in order to win this war, the U.S. government has made plans to put $500 million into the defense budget next year. Also, America is saying in the future they will establish an air base on USSR's Kamchatka and bomb the Japanese home islands.

Navy Secretary Knox is claiming that the day war started, it was the Japanese Fifth Fleet that attacked Pearl Harbor. English-language papers, the *Herald* and *Daily News,* are giving vivid scenes of spying activity as if they had seen it, but we Japanese just cannot believe it.

January 1, 1942

New Year came. The seventeenth year of Showa (*1942). If it were a peacetime New Year we were welcoming, we would be filled with hope, and our cheeks would be glistening with joy, but now our family has to wander in violent sea of misery and a dark and endless forest of suffering and agony.

Since going abroad in 1925, there has been no New Year filled with uncertainty and as lonely as this one. As an enemy person, we, Issei, are in a really serious, peculiar circumstances that cannot be described fully with pen or vocally. We cannot greet others with "Happy New Year." Because to us, at any moment, we do not know what kind of road of thorns, what misery will come upon us at any moment.

Nine in the morning, our household voiced sutra "shoshinge" together in front of the Buddhist altar. Only when praising the virtues of Buddha am I able to forget the pain in my soul and feel the pleasure of peacefulness. My husband and I are Japanese, and therefore thoroughly enemy nationals, twelve-year-old Yoko and ten-year-old Sachiko are American citizens who are recipients of the blood of the enemy; and Tokuhisa and Kazuo who are studying at Tokyo at Shiba Middle School because they have U.S. citizenship and in Japan, in the opposite way, will be treated as the enemy and must be undergoing hardship. When I think of each of those things thoroughly, it feels like I am having a terrible nightmare, and my head becomes dazed, and I cannot think straight.

I ate the traditional New Year's rice cake soup which had no taste, and in the afternoon, I visited Mr. Sei Fujii, president of the *Kashu Mainichi* (Japanese-English newspaper in Los Angeles). He has high blood pressure, and his health is so-so. When I came home, we had five visitors by nightfall.

Today's radio said, "At present, Prime Minister Churchill is discussing with President Roosevelt how to make trouble for Japan. And Churchill is waiting for the arrival of Stalin."

Discussions to make trouble for Japan—I wonder what that might be. My heart shudders! My husband and I had our wrinkles of distress increased by one. Brilliant strategist Churchill will try to get results for his country by spilling the least amount of blood of English soldiers. If Japan is bombed, it will retaliate, so what will happen to Los Angeles?

Since the war broke out, it has been twenty-plus days; I prayed in my heart and thought many times, but there is no way to deny that at the bottom of my heart, there are two lumps that cannot be softened. But it is because I am Japanese that I agonize about this, but I cannot speak of it. The reason is that it might generate harm from angry countrymen. Japan, which has prided itself of Bushido, conveyed from the ancient past. Why did it voluntarily and with one stroke initiate action that trampled it into the dirt? To behead someone who is sleeping is a shameful act. Make your sword stroke from the front, was that a lie? Really, to pick a day of rest, a Sunday before daylight, what is this about launching an attack on the sleeping?

When I am reproached about this by Americans, I have to bear shame that is similar to death. But I also in my heart try to believe— Japan may have had no other choice. And yet why did Japan have to perform an act as stupid as a praying mantis taking on an axe? I would like to ask.

The other is, since this war was going to be launched, it can be said the people involved must have intended to pound Japanese countrymen in America and including Ambassadors Nomura and Kurusu as human poles into the ground. From the standpoint of killing a little bug to allow a big bug to live, it must be considered the natural thing to do. However, regardless of whether one has any desire to volunteer to become a casualty, we have all to the last person become discarded people.

Saying that, my true love for my motherland has not changed. And on the other hand, my love for this America where I have lived for some twenty years, where I was prepared to be buried and where until this war broke out I was happy when I think of my second home country, there is confusion and more confusion, and I can only tremble in the dark confusion.

Ah, if it comes to this, under a Japanese bomb, even if I die, I can only resign myself to it being fated destiny. I will leave everything to come what may; if I am to die, I will probably die; if I am to live, then I may live. I can only do what mortals do and leave fate to heaven.

Until today I have experienced various hardships, but this is the first time I have been declared the enemy and hurled into the trial of suffering for my sins of a prior life.

Today, again, two Japanese were stabbed by lawless Koreans. Walking alone at night is dangerous. Afternoon thunderstorms and terrible weather.

January 2

From morning the roar of airplanes. Uneasy feeling fills my breast like a bat spreading its black wings and doesn't move. "Japan is too strong," read the headlines in the English-language newspaper, so it must have been a shock. The newspapers and radio are reporting Germany is recently suffering defeats. Last night, the radio reported that after a small battle, the Russians captured six hundred prisoners, so the local German people are very worried.

January 3

The temperature dropped sharply, but clear skies came. Today, again, many airplanes were flying, making very loud noises.

To ease this loneliness, this suffering, I started a major cleanup of the kitchen. I thought if I really did a lot of hard labor, I would be able to get away from this agony, but it was a big mistake. For instance, amidst a strong fatigue like the completely broken bubbling white of an egg, immeasurable anguish like turbulent waves engulfed me, and I somehow felt like groaning in a loud voice. On the cold linoleum floor of the kitchen, with folded skirt under my knees, with big sighs, my tears dropped like hot water.

I had four guests. We have *mochi*, so I made *zoni* (rice cake soup) and served each one.

My husband, since we entered the New Year, has been painting. We were asked by a neighbor parent (parent of a student) that there is a lady who wants to rent a room from the middle of this month, so we agreed. We cleared up a room we had used for a classroom for lower grades, laid carpet, and put in a bed. We painted the bedroom and window sills a light green, and it came out beautiful. That room had a kitchen of its own.

We lived in this house for over three years, but we thought the kitchen was a large closet. We learned this was a kitchen by chance about two weeks before the war started. So we removed the chairs and bed parts the landlord had shoved in there and painted it white, and it became a bright and clean kitchen. There was a white ceramic sink, and the gas was connected. So this house has three kitchens, three bathrooms, and nine separate rooms. Downstairs, it had two porches, upstairs had a hallway, and there was a three-car garage and two yards. They say a wealthy Jewish person built it, but it is completely run down. But it is not bad to have memories of once in your life having lived in such a large house. Since losing our jobs, we have been a doing thorough cleaning, so the inside of the house has cleaned up considerably. But even though the place would get dirty, I cherish the memories of students going in and out and living a vibrant and active life.

In the evening, our neighbor, Reporter Itami, came over and said, "Please write again from Monday. Stay away from current problems . . ."

Since the war, anyway the activities of the Communists have been rampant, and I am one of those who are hated by them, so I could encounter disaster at any time. On top of that, as something written by a foreigner from an enemy country, what I write will be exposed to the public; it is really a headache inducing work. In order to minimize injury, I will definitely have a number of people read it and ask for critique and only then put it in print. But this work too will probably not last long.

Today the announcement banning sale of automobiles came out. The four hundred fifty thousand currently in the inventory of retailers, the two hundred thousand that will be produced during January, this total of six hundred fifty thousand will be considered for takeover by the government for delivery to foreign countries, for use by the government, and for official use by the Civil Defense Department, and all sales of new cars to citizens will be prohibited. And they say in the future private automobiles may also be taken.

Today President Roosevelt denied Stalin was visiting the United States. He is a person who is a riddle to the world. He is an international mystery. Prime Minister Churchill said something to the effect that Stalin would be flying to the United States, but this is about the seemingly mysterious Stalin. I didn't think he was the type that would easily get up and come visit, and I was right.

Since the attack on Manila by the Japanese military, uncultured XX people have attacked Japanese at a number of locations. Residents of Brawley, Mr. Nanatsugu (?) Kikuchi (age sixty) and his wife (age forty) were assaulted on New Year's Eve and with a pistol by thugs and met tragic deaths. In El Centro, on the thirtieth of last month, two Japanese youth from Salinas at a pool hall on Broadway were shot by a pistol and hospitalized. The home of Mr. Tachibara in Santa Maria was shot into, but no one was injured. The homes of farmers in Gilroy, Mr. Ouchida and neighbor Mr. Matsumoto, were fired into on New Year's Day, and Mr. Ouchida (age thirty-seven) was wounded in the head and Matsumoto Matsuo (age ten) in the thigh. Mr. Shigaki Kosaku of Costa Mesa on the night of the thirtieth had five rounds fired into his house, but no one was injured. In the city of Los Angeles, Issei Mr. Nagase, who lives on 503 First Street, was assaulted by four thugs before dawn on the second and had several front teeth broken and was robbed of his alien registration and $47. These incidents were reported in the newspaper.

The sad darkness that lies ahead only continues to increase. It has become as if the figure of Amida (Buddha) wrapped in bright lights is nowhere to be seen.

It was announced that "enemy aliens turn in guns and Japanese swords to the nearest police station and to get a permit to travel outside the city." We don't have any guns or swords, so there is no need to turn anything in, but not being able to travel outside the city, we will be unable to have someone give us a ride to go outside the neighborhood.

January 4

To the *Kashu Mainichi*, I wrote an article, "The Position of the Issei," but under the circumstances, I asked that my name be left out, but what will happen?

We Japanese have become the enemy. We have to act with special care and avoid harm—I wrote frankly about that.

Today's news in the *Los Angeles Times* reported about Dr. Phillips who had spent many years in China as a missionary, who had returned to the United States recently, saying the following:

> "Japanese soldiers, they raped twenty-seven thousand Chinese girls between the ages of eleven to fifteen, and then they poured oil on them and burned them alive. The conduct of Japanese soldiers is unforgivable. I have brought home one thousand feet of film on what the Chinese are going through, and I intend to show those films and go around lecturing . . ."

This is really shocking! However, just how much of it is really true? For Americans, this kind of report will raise the will to fight—but for us who unexpectedly have been named the enemy—like people who hang their heads for their crimes, to us timid Japanese, it is an indescribable blow. Even now, Issei-operated markets, and fruit stands have no customers.

January 5

Afternoon, I was sewing a sample form of a different children's clothes when at around four, the doorbell rang. It was two neatly dressed Americans about thirty years of age. They said, "There is something we want to ask Aoki."

They finally came. It's the FBI—one glance, and I knew! I politely invited them into the waiting room and said, "My husband is at his friend's house, so I will phone him. Please wait a moment."

I called Mr. Onodera's place, but the line was busy. I waited awhile and called again, but the line was still busy, so I called Sachiko and told her, "Go get Father from Mr. Onodera's place."

Sachiko said, "Okay." And in her cheerful way as usual, she took off, walking like she was jumping sideways, so I hurriedly ran down the front stone steps and caught up with her and in rapid Japanese told her, "They are FBI. Father is going to be investigated, so keep that in mind." She said, "*What?*" And the little girl's face that was always shining white with health suddenly went pale and turned blue, and with tears in her eyes, she took off running!

After a short while, my husband came home; and with my husband, we sat at a table facing the two Americans.

The two Americans rose slightly and said, "This is who we are." And they opened their coat and showed us their FBI badges and let loose their first arrow of questions.

"Are you the secretary of the Toyama Prefecture Association?"

My husband said yes, and after that, he was asked in detail about names of members, addresses, association by-laws, and association president.

We had heard from earlier that one hundred forty missionary families that had spent many years in Japan had returned to the United States as soon as relations became strained, and the majority of them are now working as FBI agents, and many are fluent in Japanese. Therefore, we must be careful in not speaking half-understood English and making a mistake.

Yoko was calmly standing behind us, but Sachiko was in the corner of the room and from time to time looking up with terrified eyes and looking at us and the FBI agents and shivering like a little bird being glared at by a hawk.

The FBI agent in the black suit was writing down what we were saying to each other. *Aha, this person must be fluent in Japanese*, so I thought, and my nerves were on edge. The one asking questions one after another was the one in the gray suit, and the one in the black suit only wrote and almost never spoke, but from time to time, there was a slight change of expression. Gray suit was very tactful, and in moments between conversations would take out his cigarette case and offer a cigarette to my husband. When they finished asking questions, they came with "We would like to search your home. Can we do that?"

We answered, "Yes, anywhere you please." They started searching the living room, the front classroom, and the bedrooms upstairs as they pleased. They found a reel put away in the upstairs bureau and said, "You must have films. Bring it out." I brought out the three reels— *Samurai Japan, Riptide,* and *Rice*—I brought back last year when I visited my two sons in Japan. I had shown it to my students as a gift.

While I was getting the films, Yoko was carefully watching the FBI agents. She whispered to me, "Mother, that black-suited FBI was reading the middle school Chinese classics text you use to teach. And from Mother's large notebook (that large notebook was related to the Hollywood school where I taught on Saturdays), he took one report card."

When they came to my husband's belongings and saw a shining, fairly large new brass case, they said, "Is there a sword or pistol in there? Open it up and let us see!" So we opened it, and a set of carpenter tools which had been used only once or twice without a spot of rust or cloud was displayed, and they laughed. My husband, thinking of making something, had bought it for $50 at Fukuyama's hardware store the day before war broke out. The investigation ended after over an hour. And they took the films and two or three books.

After that, I fixed dinner and was talking to a visitor when the doorbell rang by someone who really kept ringing it hard! When I went to see, it was two different Americans that looked like officials. This time, they were around thirty-seven or thirty-eight, large fellows, and looked ominous.

They said, "We are from . . . We want to talk to Mr. Aoki." And they took FBI badges from their pockets and showed us.

"Are you the secretary of the school association?"

"Yes."

"Show us all minutes, by-laws, and accounting ledgers."

My husband brought out the minutes and by-laws. He said, "The accounting records are at either the Chairman of the Board Shimano Sensei's place or at the institute."

They said, "In that case, come with us to Mr. Shimano's house." My husband started to go upstairs to change into a suit, but they said, "Come as you are." So I hurriedly had him change into the better suit coat in front of them.

My husband got into the FBI's gray-colored auto and went with them to Shimano Sensei's house. After searching together with Mrs. Shimano and her son, it was not found, so they went to the institute. Shimano Sensei was being detained at the Montana Detention Center, so no one knew how to open the safe.

He was told, "Tomorrow we will break it open so you can be a witness." That worried him, so he again went to Shimano Sensei's house. There, Mrs. Shimano told him, "We searched again later and found it." And he brought out the account ledger. Therefore, right away together with Mr. Shimano's son, they delivered it to the FBI office. When my husband went with the FBI agents, Sachiko said, "Is it all right for Father to ride in that car?" She was worried and had turned pale. Finally she burst out crying. When he returned, she leapt with joy. But things have come to where they have come! After they check the minutes and ledgers, it is not certain when they will come to take him away.

With a feeling that the light of salvation has turned darker and the scalpel of anguish that cuts into my soul has been sharpened, the blood in my body has turned cold and gray.

We heard that by eleven tonight, they will investigate six hundred suspected enemy aliens.

January 6

I only saw dreams, and all night long, I dozed on and off and did not sleep well. The voice of my daughters who had risen early and someone talking could be heard, so I went down from my second-floor bedroom to see. It was an early morning visitor who had come to inquire how we were after yesterday's FBI investigation. The fact that we had been investigated twice and on one visit had our place searched was already common knowledge in our community.

In my column, I titled it "Frost" and wrote about being investigated twice. Since it had come to this, there is no longer any need to conceal my name. I swear before the gods of the Heaven and Earth I have done nothing to be ashamed of.

President Roosevelt, today at thirty minutes after noon, before both houses, announced the production plan. During 1943, twelve thousand five hundred airplanes, seventy-five thousand tanks, thirty-five thousand anti-aircraft guns, and ten million tons of ships are being planned to be built. In order to accomplish that, during 1942, sixty thousand airplanes, forty-five thousand tanks, twenty-thousand anti-aircraft guns, and eight million tons of ships must be built. This proposed budget will be $56 billion, over half of the total income of all the United States.

Since January 1, the government has repeatedly said, "Do not listen to shortwave broadcasts. Japan is sending out false information." But strangely, it seems to appeal to Americans; and ironically, the sale of shortwave radios is good. The reputation of Japanese who broadcast in English is quite good, and since Americans listen to them, eventually the news comes to us. It is very strange. In the Philippines, it seems they are using currency issued by Japan. The U.S. government will soon increase government employees to four million; soldiers will be given about six months training and hurriedly sent to the front. And they say Japanese American soldiers will be sent to the European theater.

Hour by hour, it seems the tiger's mouth comes closer. I must not break down! Busily moving this body withered from anxiety, I have prepared to be taken away at any time by packing clothes and necessities in a suitcase. Yoko, while tears fill her eyes, holds in her anguish and quietly watches with a very sad expression, but Sachiko cries loudly and is rubbing her eyes from which tears flow. The sight of both her eyelids swollen light purple above her white face is very pitiful.

January 7

They say there is frost damage in places, and farmers have suffered losses. The weather bureau says, "Information on frost damage will benefit the enemy, so no forecasts on frost will be made." I wonder if that can be true.

In Utah, they say because of the fear of being attacked by XX people, all Japanese girls are collected in one house and guarded by an American public school teacher. I heard that in Guadalupe, to prepare against XX people, they have hired an American special policeman.

Today I heard a rumor that on the Shanghai Exchange; $100 is only worth ¥40. If that is the case, our wealth is worth very little. In the year of 1925 right after World War I, we invested over $12,000 cash and purchased two plots of land in a place called Manoa in Hawaii. That property, with the subsequent depression, decreased in value to a piddling amount and twice faced forced auction for nonpayment of tax, and we had considered getting rid of it.

We only thought about it and worried about it, but we couldn't decide and didn't know how to go about it, and time passed. Right at that time, we heard from Fukushimaya (Fukushima's store) in Japan town that an old lady Gypsy fortune-teller had shown up, and she would tell people about their past, present, and future as if she were pointing it out in the palm of her hand, and her reputation was very high. The owner of Fukushimaya was so impressed by her reading that in appreciation, every Thursday for Japanese customers to be seen by her, he was providing a room. Her reputation was so good that I decided to have this old lady read the fortune on this property, and it was a morning on a Thursday in May of last year that I went to see her.

After waiting for several customers to finish, I went into the room and met this old lady. Her hair was half white; on her face which was light black, as the Japanese say, was the shadow of death as on a memorial tablet. She was a shabby, dirty-looking old lady with wrinkled features on a black face that resembled a memorial tablet, and she was wearing a very loose gray dress. She had much in common with the witches of Macbeth, and only the sunken eyes were shining brightly. When I stood before her, she gave a slight nod and said, "You are a person who is always by a large desk. You are a hotel registrar, and if not, then a school teacher. And you live in a two-story house which is quite large, don't you?"

She spoke slowly with a muddled accent. I was taken slightly aback at the time. So I said, "I am not a hotel registrar."

When I spoke right away about the property problem, she closed her eyes and held her head with both hands for a while and then said, "If you try hard to sell it, this August there will be only one buyer, and if you let that get away, it will not come again. The price is very cheap. However, it is probably better to sell."

Right away, I sent the diagram of the land to an acquaintance, Mr. S, in Hawaii and asked him to sell it. Strangely enough, in August, a Chinese person said he would buy it if the price was $1,900. That is what he wrote, so we immediately sold it. We had invested the money into our school, but now having come to this, it is the same as nothing.

At the time, the fortune-telling old lady said, "Your fate is that you will have to teach your daughters until your hair is completely white."

I had not asked anything about that, so I asked, "I am thinking of writing a children's book during this year. What do you think of that?"

At that, she said, "Now is definitely not the time for that. However, among the books you write in the future, three should sell very well."

I wonder what books will sell. As long as you are going to publish a book, it is better to have one that sells rather than one that does not.

Laws prohibiting travel became gradually stricter, and they say soon we will not be able to use the train. Ah, today too, somehow, the day ended safely.

January 8

I hear that on the Shanghai Exchange, a dollar was down to ¥25, and they say it might go down to ¥10 to ¥5 and, eventually, to where it cannot be exchanged. If the dollar cheapens, the more it cheapens; the feeling of reliance on the United States by the Chinese will lessen; but on the other hand, for us Japanese in America, the hard work of half of our lives will become worthless and, just like the words say, like bubbles of water. If we stay alive, and if we ever have to someday live in Japan, until we find another occupation, we must have enough property in Japan to see us through. It is unknown when this war will end. I don't have the strength to worry about the far future. With a simple, open mind, I will go where the hands of fate lead.

In the afternoon, Reporter Itami came and said, "They say, the other day, at the theater, two Japanese American young men booed when the scene of Churchill and Roosevelt meeting was shown, and when the scene of Pearl Harbor in Hawaii being bombed came out, laughed out loud, and when an old American lady sitting behind them cautioned them, they spit on her. Therefore, the old lady sued. When the two young men showed up in court, the old lady did not attend, so the two were found innocent and released. This old lady was an old miss with a twisted mind, and she was the one who had spit. Most of the incident was a fabrication, and when I wrote an article in the English section of the *Kashu Mainichi* and titled it "BABA," the old lady protested, saying, "The word *baba* must mean 'shitty old lady,' and if you don't retract it, I will sue."

I also wrote four volumes of essays, and it was agony like having my blood squeezed out. I carefully chose each word, each phrase, and asked my husband and two or three others to review it. If they pointed out something here, I would change the wording; and if asked about, there I would explain it thusly and prepare even for after publication. Even if one is careful, if I continue writing, there is no telling what frightful involvement I could become involved in. It is common in wartime for unreasonable things to triumph over reason, and therefore, I will not write.

In thinking back until today, almost eight years, by coincidence I was discovered by President Mr. Fujii (*Kashu Mainichi* newspaper), and I lucked out in having the opportunity to write over two thousand essays, reviews, and children's stories. Even those who do not know my name know my pen name Yamamoto Asako. Readers who I cannot see supported me over a long period, especially gentle-minded farmers who said of my writing, "Ms. Asako who gives us our daily sustenance." Their love of my writing cannot be measured. In the beginning, readers who were accustomed to the spirited writing of the former writer, Reporter Mishima Akiko, would urge me to, "Please write interesting things like Akiko San."

I would reply, "You tell me that, but I can't do that. A pen has the characteristics of the holder. I am a person raised in a field of education and religion, and like my feelings, I can only wield a very simple pen. However, I may be able to write things for you to think about."

After a while, it became, "If you eat sushi every day, you will tire of it. Asako San, your writing is like rice. Please continue writing forever and become the sustenance for our soul," and, "When I receive the *Kashu Mainichi*, the first thing I read is your column!"

Oh, *Kashu Mainichi*, good-bye! When the war is over, and if I am alive at that time, it is not impossible that the day that I write again will not come again! I will keep one pleasant hope alive.

Until today, a total of four FBI agents have come to our house and took all sorts of records. If they investigate those and we are to be taken away, it should be around next Monday—we think so, and friends also tell us that is a possibility. This Monday, they took away twelve people, and it seems a total of one thousand six hundred have been confined thus far. What an uneasy, melancholy daily existence.

Eating meals is like biting into sand and completely tasteless! I hear that two hundred fifty-plus people connected to the Consulate in Hawaii were all confined at one time. They say it is because they found a person using lights to let the Japanese know when a warship come in or goes out from Pearl Harbor. Probably because of that, a warning went out that Japanese are not allowed to have flashlights. The battery had gone out in the one in our house, so we took a hammer and destroyed it.

The other day, there was a large work stoppage at a fish factory in San Pedro, and they say tonight or tomorrow, the Los Angeles trolley system will have a work stoppage. Whenever there is a strike, Americans say it may be the work of Axis Fifth Columnists, so it becomes unbearable. When I think about it, we who loved America so much and if asked, compared to our motherland Japan which is better, we couldn't answer right away because the scale in our mind was equally balanced; and from the standpoint of education and religion, we had preached and written that one must perform good deeds. And I myself lived with that in mind and stressed in teaching students, "You are born with the blood of Japanese who have had pride from ancient times. Train yourselves and become the best American citizens."

Just what crime did we commit that we must live in fear of being arrested? My husband simply says, "It is because we are at war." Even if one says it is war, it is like a bolt out of the blue and has not one iota of my intentions that caused it. Furthermore, because of that we Japanese in America have become outcasts to Japan, and to America we have become the enemy. Can there be any position as trying? After deep mental agony, I thought, *Then, as a Japanese, to be born at this time is my lot for sins committed in a prior life.*

In the evening, I had a visitor. We talked.

"Singapore, when it gets to be, April will be the rainy season, and there will really be heavy rain, and it will just become a muddy mire. When that happens, war will become difficult. It would be nice if it fell. The earlier the better."

January 9

It is one month since the war started. In newly occupied Japanese territory, Japanese flags must be flapping in the wind.

It seems the strike of trolleys and city busses will take place at the end of May. They say if increased pay is agreed to before that, there will be no strike.

America's top class commentator Lippmann is saying, "For America to plan on only production of weapons and not control everyday commodities and try to win the war is a mistake."

To repeatedly say to buy defense bonds is for the government to collect money and prevent bad inflation, but the price of commodities continue to rise. The price of a sack of rice which was $5 something before the war is now $10. I am shocked a gallon of Kikkoman shoyu is $3.50. I am totally astonished on the price which knows no limit of Japanese goods. It is because they cannot be supplied.

Communist paper, with the following reasoning, says, "They say the Filipinos attack the Japanese, but Filipinos are Americans, and Japanese are the enemy, so it can't be helped." When I think the viewpoint of the dastardly communists are all this ridiculous, we must exterminate these deadly bugs as soon as we can.

The word that Mr. and Mrs. Aoki were arrested is widespread. No matter who looks at it, my husband and I are probably among those to be taken in. Even if I am to be confined, I do not want to go to Montana where one has to go through a winter at minus 20 degrees. I am sensitive to cold.

January 10

At the confinement center for enemy aliens in New York, Germans really hate being confined with Japanese because they say, "We are superior human beings than the Japanese."

January 11

From morning to evening, there were thirteen guests. Mrs. Tanaka said, "Last night, I dreamt about you. I wondered how you were doing and came to visit." She came in a car hauling a large box filled with candies and fruits.

She said, "We are a store, so we have about thirty sacks of rice stacked up. Whenever you are in need of groceries, we will provide it, so please do not hesitate to speak up." I wasn't hurting for foodstuff, but tears welled up when I heard those words of consideration.

How many years hence will it be before peace comes, and we can take up the problem of reopening our Japanese-language school? The other day, when Endo Koshiro Sensei visited, he looked so dejected when he painfully said, "Alas, it is futile. Until today, I have funneled in $30,000, but having come to this, I give up."

I sighed and said, "We haven't put in a fraction of what you have, but it's over."

He said, "Even at that, you have four children. From the standpoint of people like me who haven't even one child, you are fortunate . . ." So saying, it appeared as if he was wiping tears. That's to be expected. Over a long period, the school that husband and wife spent all their efforts in building had, with one blow, been wiped out. Words like regret and mortification do not begin to describe the feeling.

Evening, Ms. M who had applied for renting a room came. She was a quiet, composed, refined young lady and gave one the feeling of coming in contact with, for instance, a celadon porcelain incense burner. Her father had already been confined and presently in Montana. My two children were very happy saying, "Big sister had arrived." It was a pretty large room with a kitchen. Everyone says it should be all right to get $15, but we are renting the space to reduce our rent, so I said, $8. However, the other party said, "That is too cheap. Let me pay $10." For us who have lost all income, a dollar today is like $3 before the war.

Today, from one visitor, I heard that a jobless Japanese family of three tried to commit suicide. Tragedies only increase. For us, what will develop tomorrow? My chest hurts with an agony that feels like it is cutting into my heart.

January 12

All Japanese families, they say, are being investigated by the FBI. Therefore, my husband said, he has decided to destroy the ten thousand feet of film he had stored in someone else's storage room. It had some footage concerning the war in China, so now that it has come to this; they are not desirable. I asked my children, "Please help us." "Yes." And the four of us sat on the rug in the bedroom each with a box in front and with scissors cut it into small pieces.

The whole family was enveloped with sadness and without the energy to even talk, remained silent. The film we are pulling out from the boxes, from time to time, snags and makes a dreary sound and gives a strange, cold feeling. When we finished cutting, my husband and I took it to the downstairs bathroom and flushed it a little bit at a time. However, the last time we flushed it, the water came back and overflowed and flooded the bathroom. "Now we have a problem!"

My husband and I looked at each other with faces turned pale. We brought the hand-operated pump with funnel-shaped rubber pipe that we used whenever the toilet, wash machine, and sink were plugged up, and each in turn stuck it in and tried, but the water would not drain. If we push with all our might, the harder we push in reverse proportion, the water would flow back. We are in a real bind!

With the passage of time, we will have to use the bathroom. If we do that, filth will flow back. Now that it has come to this, we felt there was no other way than to call a Japanese plumber, explain what happened, and have the film removed. Anyway, our house was large, the pipes were buried and ran every which way under the floor, and it became a major project and took over half a day and was an unexpected expense. The film was all faded white, and the pictures could not be made out, but the shape was the same as when we cut it, and about enough to fill a large bucket and a half came out. The plumber looked surprised and said, "No matter what, that was overdoing things!"

And he went home. Since it was films, we couldn't burn it, and thus it came to this. We took that and dug a hole near the high wall bordering our Mexican neighbor and buried it.

At present, America is saying we are sending large numbers of soldiers to Europe; and once we defeat Hitler, it is a given that Japan, which is an underling of Germany, will naturally lose and therefore in the Pacific war, do not have any expectations. Oh, Japan is an underling of Germany? A wry smile is evoked. At a time when the world countries are all tied up in wars and tired, the only ruler is the emperor of Japan who embodies the honorable bloodline of three thousand years of rule in Asia—so said Dr. Einstein. We are the children of heaven. We are by no means underlings of Germany!

January 13

During the morning, I went to the telephone office and paid an additional $4.50 deposit. Because this morning I received a phone call from the phone company saying Japanese, German, and Italian enemy foreigners all lose their jobs and probably end up unable to pay their phone bills, so they must pay an additional deposit of $4.50 by today or tomorrow. Our school is closed, and I no longer write for the newspaper, so we are completely jobless. So even if our phone is disconnected, it doesn't matter; but without a phone, it is inconvenient. So as long as we stay in this house, we will leave the phone connected.

This morning's paper said courts will not accept cases brought by enemy aliens, so does that mean we cannot sue even if illegally assaulted and injured? If that is true, using that as an opportunity, unlawful non-Japanese will attack us. Japanese must individually protect themselves and avoid danger by being careful.

A professor at the University of California said, "It is futile to bomb Tokyo now. Persevere for a while, and during that time, America must prepare ample airplanes, tanks, battleships, etc., and when all is ready, use thousands of airplanes and bomb Japan every thirty minutes and completely destroy every Japanese city."

At the confinement center, it seems the investigation of those who were confined as enemy alien have started. Today there was an article in the newspaper like this:

> "Investigation of Enemy Aliens Begins. Among the first to be determined as necessary to be confined by the local Enemy Alien Hearing Board, and after investigation after confinement, German lady Stephani Hoehenrohe Schlingfaust (?) was determined to be a dangerous enemy alien and should be confined until the war is over, and

that opinion was forwarded to Attorney General Biddle.
This woman was born of Hungarian parents and married
an Austrian noble but was known from before of having
close connections with the German Nazi League. In 1938,
she came to the United States as an advisor to Capt. Fritz
Weidman at the German General Consulate in San Francisco.
And when Captain Weidman was declared persona non grata
and left, she was under surveillance as a dangerous person."

It seems six Japanese were investigated. There is no Japanese who
operated as a spy; therefore, if investigated closely, the majority should
be allowed to return home. In any event, that is what I hope.

They say that ever since Japan attacked the Dutch East Indies,
the import of raw rubber from that area has ceased; so to meet the
demands of the military and civilian usage, they set up a plan to produce
four hundred thousand tons of synthetic rubber. It is estimated that
compared to the cost of 20¢ a pound for raw rubber, synthetic rubber
will cost 30¢ a pound. This synthetic rubber is made from crude oil,
but they say it is inferior to natural rubber.

Since it is war time, the construction of storage for agricultural
products, dairies, poultry houses will be allowed, but ordinary residences
will not be allowed. They say the construction of automobile garages
might be allowed if metal pipes and nails are not used. For the past ten
years, America exported scrap iron to Japan; and now when for defense
purposes major increases in production is planned, there is a shortage
of scrap iron. And even if it is recovered from farms and automobile
junkyards, it may not be enough. The agency in charge of National
Defense Production is in dire straits.

The heavyweight boxing champion of the world, Joe Louis,
volunteered and joined the army. Wendell Willkie will be appointed as

the head of the newly established Wartime Labor Bureau. Since the war started, time has gone by, but the American public has yet to get the feeling that we are at war. The usual easygoing, broad-minded attitude must be the cause. Only the government seems to be making every effort to raise the fighting spirit.

January 14

During the morning hours from around nine, for about an hour my husband, together with representatives of the Japanese school association, Sugimachi, Yoshizumi, Hoshimiya, three school heads, had a meeting in our reception room since it had been decided to call on Public Prosecutor Palmer about the Japanese school problem. After that, they went to the farmer's (?) building and met with the public prosecutor.

He kindly explained, "There is no law that says you cannot teach Japanese. But this is a bad time to reopen Japanese schools. Please write to the education bureau of each state and ask for details."

At this time, is civil disturbance going to take place in Germany? The Red Forces are talking about a winter offensive. That Japanese Forces are winning is obvious from American newspapers, reporting, "No change in the war situation." If Japanese Forces have even a slight reversal, headlines would read, "Japs lose!" Today's paper was filled with articles on "Is the Puzzling Civil Disturbance in Germany Coming Soon?" "An Isolated Hitler Desperate to Raise More Troops."

Since the start of the war, America has been severely hurting for rubber and tin. Rubber needs are being met with synthetic rubber, and they say tin will be obtained from discarded cans. For an America that prided itself on having ample quantities of all commodities, to have to resort to collecting discarded cans is unprecedented. "Ah, this kind of age too has come." It feels a bit strange.

January 15

The word that Japan's XX *Maru* was sunk is going around. Please, I hope it is not true. Wherever I go, I am looked upon as the enemy by stern eyes. Ah, when it has come to this, I would rather return to Japan.

January 16

Today people came and told me that at the confinement center, Dr Honda cut his wrist and committed suicide. Can it be true, or is it a rumor? If it is true, it is truly so sad!

At one time, the doctor said, "War between Japan and the United States will never happen. If by misfortune it does occur, two tigers will both be harmed. I think those governing Japan know this. The reason I organized Japanese veterans into a Veterans Friendship Organization was so that we veterans in the United States could emphasize that we must not go to war and do our small bit for peace."

Now unfortunately, that war between Japan and the United States which should not happen did happen. And members of that Veterans Friendship Group were the first to be arrested, so it is not unthinkable that the doctor felt responsible and committed suicide. In the evening paper, I learned the doctor committing suicide was not a lie. In any event, war produces casualties in unexpected places. I had heard the doctor was an ardent Christian, but we lit a candle in front of our family Buddhist altar and intoned a Buddhist sutra for him.

January 17

Morning, my husband, with Yoshizumi Sensei, took a copy written in English of what Public Prosecutor Palmer said to three Japanese-language newspapers. After returning, he took the children to buy shoes; and just during his absence, the head of the Compton Japanese Language School, Endo Sensei, came and in a completely dejected manner asked, "What happened with negotiations with the authorities?"

Sensei, who lived until today treasuring his school next to his life, since losing his hope, appeared to have aged five or six years at once. We gloomily talked mixing sighs for about an hour and waited, but Husband did not return, so Sensei appeared even more disappointed, saying, "Then I will go home." And he stood up. I said, "In any event, this morning with Yoshizumi Sensei, the two of them took it to the newspaper company, so the detail should come out in the newspaper. Please read it there."

There is a rumor that Japanese will be chased into the inlands in March, April, so Issei are completely depressed. Gradually becoming an urgent situation are the Japanese families that have lost their jobs. I heard of a couple who only had a block of tofu for a side dish for three days. How sad!

January 18

It appears the USSR might enter into a separate peace treaty with Germany, thus the United States has nervously announced.

It was in the *Times* that the Compton School head, Endo Sensei, who visited yesterday, was arrested on a warrant by the president. The reason was not written, but the writing generated the feeling that an important enemy alien had been caught. In any event, it seems he was taken as soon as he returned from my place, and I could clearly picture

Sensei in his confused state of mind, and I felt overcome with fear and uncertainty that made my blood run cold.

When I said, "If a ship came for me, I will throw everything away and return to Japan with only what I have on and start over."

He sadly said, "Even if I return to Japan, I would be lost . . ." He also said, "With me, and I believe it is the same with you, even if we are without work, we are not the type to work for others, so it is very difficult. I am thinking about living on $15 a month."

Investing $30,000 of his own money, his Compton Japanese Language School which was said to be more beautiful than public schools in the area, this Sensei who had such high spirits and dashing manner, talking in such a timid manner, my feelings too felt like they were being pushed into darkness. We had received large silver trays from Japan's Education Association as awards for Overseas Education, but most of it was not working in Japan, so even though we had been teaching for over twenty years, there was no pension. For a teacher, there is probably nothing less rewarding as teaching in a Japanese school in America.

Recently, there is talk of sending all Japanese children over seven years of age to New Mexico and let them live there. Should that happen, it means lifelong parting with my two daughters. Even if I have to live hand to mouth, I want to live with my children.

January 19

At the vegetable wholesale market, white Americans are trying to take away Issei's businesses and give it to other races.

To us who have become the enemy, each day everything becomes difficult. Until the war ends, just what kind of life do we have to endure? Now over a month since the war started, America, which valued

Japanese farmers highly, is attempting to change that to Mexicans and Filipinos. The Japanese-language paper reported that an old Japanese had committed suicide because of living difficulties.

January 20

Ms. Fujii of Taiheiyo Sewing School said, "It seems Reporter Kato of *Sangyo Daily* was taken in for broadcasting from Japan when he returned there. You must be careful because you did the same thing."

However, there is no way for me to be careful. I can only leave it to fate. I didn't say even the slightest bad thing about America; there is nothing I have to be ashamed of. Rather, in my draft, I had written that on the trains (in Japan), the men occupied the seats as if that was the natural thing to do, and women would be standing hanging on to the leather straps; and having lived in America for many years, this felt strange; and when told to delete that page, I was taken aback.

This evening, in place of my brother-in-law, young man Mr. O delivered a wooden box full of fruits. At that time, the young man said, "Japanese broadcast is saying if one Japanese in America is killed, seven POWs will be killed."

Shining light is with those who suffer—I know those words, but it seems the sight of Buddha has become so distant, so faint. I want to be blessed with real happiness.

They say a sixty-eight-year-old German lady has been sentenced to ten years imprisonment for listening to a shortwave radio. It seems detectives are constantly going around in a vehicle with a device that has a needle that goes haywire when they near any house with a shortwave radio on, so even if you have the volume on so low it cannot be heard outside, they can tell right away.

January 21

From before daylight, airplanes are noisily flying. There are wishful rumors that because the third son of the president is a prisoner of the Japanese, the love for his son will keep the president from treating the Japanese in America too harshly. Of course, the truth of all this is unknown.

The newspaper had an article that an exchange of diplomats could be done using a Chilean ship. The Japanese are envious of the diplomats. But they are the ones who will have to work very hard after the war, so it must be that their lives must be preserved. But I feel diplomats in the postwar world must be blood type O and of bilious character, having lived overseas for many years, and what I felt keenly disappointed about was that those diplomats who we relied upon to defend us are so cowardly and at times appeared servile. Aren't there any female diplomats who are young, pretty, quick-witted, and very active? Who can say that in the postwar diplomatic world such a woman will not appear?

In my mind, I can see any number of imagined scenes of such a person performing. But once the vision has been erased, we have the reality of this life—which is too hard and unbearable.

Does living as if one has stepped on the tail of a tiger continue for long? It has been only two months since the war started, but already it feels as if has been many years.

January 22

In the garden, large purple roses are starting to bloom. It is about the size of a peony flower. It has many rose buds, and the fragrance of roses fills the area. The image of a flower that seems to sing of the joy of the purity of life unexpectedly softens my heart, and I feel something like poetic sentiment filling my breast. The constant marching forward of nature, with total disregard to the brutal death struggle of mankind, continues on to eternity. If this was peacetime, tasting the feeling of early spring to its utmost, I may have been formulating thoughts on writing a good essay. But now, there is no happiness, no enjoyment, and peacefulness has passed us with the speed of a passing devil and anxiety, and darkness and misery bind us, so we cannot move.

At this time, Japan is in its coldest season, and one is closed in by snow and ice; but in Southern California, which is called the world's greenhouse, it is so warm we do not even need a heater.

In the afternoon, Mrs. M came to visit. She said, "Stock up on about two months' supply of food——and it should be canned goods and things that can be eaten right away."

She said that, so I purchased about $15–$16 worth of canned corn and corned beef, pickled shallot, salted salmon, milk, flour, and various other foodstuff.

Pickled *ume* (Japanese apricot) is 5¢ each and limited to ten per person. One can only be shocked by the rising price of Japanese goods. It seems there are merchants who have the same nature as arsonists and thieves. Even though countrymen, it is too contemptible. At a time like this, to feel they will lose out if they don't make even 1¢ more is pitiful.

Today's paper said a bill has been passed by the legislature to remove those with dual citizenship from government and public positions. Also, a bill proposing that without regard to citizenship, forbidding the carrying of knives, etc., has been presented to the Los Angeles City Council. This is welcome news for us enemy nationals because the possibility of being stabbed on the street by Filipinos and unknown Koreans will lessen. However, this announcement will be somewhat a problem for me because from now on, I will not be able to carry my large scissors used for sewing along with my other sewing tools.

The English-language paper said there is no indication yet that Singapore will fall, but can that be true?

January 23

When I got up in the morning, I prayed the day would hurriedly end. Living every day overwhelmed with insults and indignation and uncertainty was unbearable torture.

For emergency, in the backyard I buried three large mountain taro, over fifty carrots, over forty Japanese radishes, over thirty burdocks, two *sho* (approximately three liters) of taro. Four or five days ago, using a bucket, I distributed over a hundred heads of cabbage and fifty bunches of spinach I had received to seven neighbors.

To have neighboring farmers giving us lots of vegetables is something unimaginable to those living around Tokyo. They come with a truckload and pile it up on the porch or leave a load at the classroom, so at times, our entire household is busy delivering it around.

Since the start of the war, those arrested as endangering peace and order are 3,557 Japanese, 2,087 Germans, 243 Italians, a total of 5,887. It is strange that the reason given for the large number of Japanese arrested when they do not even comprise of one tenth of the Germans and Italians in the population was given as "the spy activities of the Japanese is more dangerous than that of Nazi Germany, and because it was done mainly through their consulate and in peacetime, they could not be arrested." It is beyond comprehension to believe there was any Japanese-spying activity. If they are thoroughly investigated, I don't believe there is even one spy among those arrested. How can one be a spy if they are so dense as to get caught? Thinking about it from various points, it's probably not wrong that Japanese are the least suitable to engage in spy activities.

January 26

Since news that by Friday of last week Japanese forces had come within twenty-five miles of Singapore, there has been no news. I wonder what the situation is.

Today the sea is covered with deep fog. During the morning broadcast at seven, they said a suspicious aircraft had come within three hundred nautical miles out in the Pacific Ocean, so all radio broadcasts will be suspended because of fear of interception. Until twelve noon, all radio broadcasts were stopped.

They say the United States has sent six or twelve divisions to Iceland in the North, and among those being sent to Europe, there must be some Japanese American soldiers.

January 27

The dome of city hall was completely hidden by heavy fog. My husband went to the citizen's association office to sign the declaration closing Japanese-language schools for the duration to submit to the army, navy, federal authorities. Representatives are Sugimachi, Yoshizumi, Hoshimiya, and Aoki—the four of them.

Recently, my husband's name would be mentioned so often in the papers; relatives and friends are worried. There are some who say, "If you sign, you will be taken."

My husband said, "It has come to this, and I will not run or hide. If they come to take me, that is that." And he went to sign.

Around noon, one of the students' parents came and said, "Please remove our child's name from the school register."

He says it is because one English-language paper said students who have been attending Japanese-language schools will be investigated.

The paper said sugar is being used to make explosives, so from next month, it will be reduced to three pounds a week per person.

It seems thirty-seven Nisei who work at various departments in city hall have been notified by the personnel manager that after two weeks, they will all be let go. It is like water in a sleeping person's ear . . . . They say the citizen's committee is making a lot of noise. The few remaining also don't know when they will be fired.

It hasn't been many days since an announcement criticizing President and Mrs. Roosevelt and Attorney General Biddle for their racially discriminatory treatment came out, so this kind of unreasonable treatment is unforgivable. Nisei are not enemy nationals. However, in the end, unless they change their face or unless they have White blood, they must walk this road of thorns with the Issei.

January 28

It cleared up, but the temperature went down a little. Concerning whether Japanese were going to be moved to inland areas of Utah, Wyoming, Arizona, Texas, etc., it seems there is debate taking place around Mayor Bowron (mayor of Los Angeles). There is an opinion that it will take place in Hawaii because the activities of fifth columnists there by Japanese were so remarkable.

This morning, at Izumio Photo Studio, I had photos made for my enemy alien registration card. It was $1.03 for a set of four photos. The 3¢ is for tax, but recently, the only ones making money are photographers, and they say there are many days when there are about two hundred taking pictures.

We will have to live off of what money we have for who knows how many years and may have to return penniless to Japan.

They say the FBI comes to get you from 4:00 p.m. to around 10:00 p.m., so when four o'clock comes, I get restless; and when it becomes ten, tension goes up. With a feeling of will they come today or will they come tomorrow, I can only eat one bowl of rice, but when ten o'clock pasts, my "suddenly getting hungry" is a funny phenomenon.

If I walk in town, I get continuous cold stares. Looking as if one had put clothes on money, two very dolled-up Jewish ladies with large eyes glared at me. In my mind, I said to myself, *Did I do something bad to you two? If you stare like that, doesn't it make you even more indecent? More than that, when you die, in the spirit world where they tally up your life in the ledger of your lifetime sins, although it may be a small amount, won't it increase the count?*

January 29

I awoke dreaming of two splendid foxes guarding our front gate. It was as if they had become guardian deities, and I thought it was strange. They are not allowing suspicious persons to enter, so I am thankful. Even if I cannot see them with my eyes, if in fact it was true, I would be so happy.

Around two in the afternoon, from the Hollywood Japanese School representing the mothers' association, Secretary Mrs. Hoshiko came bringing twenty pounds of sugar and six canned goods to report that the mothers' association had decided to dissolve. Even if the war ends, Japanese-language education in America is over. And further, it is probably fine not to teach Japanese. Motherland Japan has taken on vast new areas. As they are cultivated to implant Japanese language cannot be said is not a task remaining for us. Today, when the fruits of living abroad has burst like a bubble and the time to return to Japan arrives, in a Japan where we do not have any foundation, my spirit is too broken to work alongside prominent women in Japan.

The radio at 5:00 p.m. announced that by February 24, enemy alien Japanese, German, and Italians will be removed from areas around military installation to inland areas over fifty miles away. We in Los Angeles too, sooner or later, will probably walk this same fate. If it comes to that, we will be able to take only necessities. Now it is futile to be fixated on material things. If it has come to this, we can go on with what cannot be burned or melted by fire or water—one's skill and ability. Getting emotional must be avoided.

Fifty-six public Nisei men and women employees were relieved all at the same time. When we are moved inland, there will be no distinction of Issei and Nisei. It is all persons with Japanese blood. In front of a law without emotion, we can only bow our heads and sigh deeply.

January 30

These days, what worries Japanese is relocating inland. Today orders came out that Japanese, Germans, and Italians must vacate San Francisco in Northern California and in Southern California, Hawthorne and Inglewood by February 24.

They say they will chase us out of twenty-nine military districts located in eight states (California, Oregon, Washington, Nevada, Montana, Idaho, Utah, Arizona). The aforementioned locations must have been made examples. It is expected that areas with military facilities, Terminal Island, Downey, Santa Monica, and Burbank areas will be ordered to evacuate with certainty; but at present, this Los Angeles area is not certain. Further, they say the remaining twenty-seven areas will be announced today or tomorrow; so by Sunday, our fate will be decided. It hasn't been announced how we are to be relocated, but they say Japanese in the Hawthorne, Inglewood area number 300 households.

January 31

With the story of relocating inland, the Japanese community is on pins and needles. Even a small farmer, if it comes to moving, will need at least a thousand dollars. Since the war, many farmers have stopped planting. Even if they did plant, without fertilizer, there is no telling how it will grow. Those nurseries that were operating on a large scale, when it comes to this, all is lost, so the product of many tens of years will all be gone in one stroke. No matter what you say, those engaged in business will suffer the most. Even with ordinary households, since the circumstances are known, household goods and furniture will end up being sold dirt cheap.

Today there was an announcement of twenty-seven additional districts where enemy aliens were not allowed to enter and that sixty-nine other areas would be so designated. Los Angeles city limits have not yet been announced, but they say on Monday, seventeen other areas would be added, so it is possible it may be included. In this California, there are ninety-three thousand plus Japanese and Japanese Americans, so what will happen to these people I can't possibly guess. In an agony like being dragged into a bottomless, deep canyon, my head and my body ache. Whether we are relocated inland or arrested, we must have underwear and pajamas ready, so I bought sturdy material and until evening sewed the children's garments.

There is a loud howling of a cat in heat. In the feline world, they do fight, but it is nice they do not go to war.

February 2

My husband and I went to the Alien Registration Office. There were four policemen on guard. It is only a little after opening hour of eight, but there are many people there. There are Germans and Italians, but Japanese make up the majority. Two copies of draft form, three photos, and fingerprint was taken of the index finger. Unlike Japanese seals, it is not placing the finger flat but placing your finger lightly on and then rolling it from right to left, so it ends up clearly square. Then we went to another room, and information from the draft is filled in on a small purple-colored identification booklet. The person taking care of me was a secretary-type white woman of about thirty wearing glasses.

"How tall are you?"

"Five feet four inches."

"Weight?"

"One hundred pounds."

"Outstanding characteristic?"

"All dentures."

There were three or four questions like this, and we were finished in about thirty minutes. On the way home, a portly refined white woman over fifty approached and asked, "Was the registration office unpleasant?"

I answered, "It wasn't like that." She said, "I am German." While we are both the same enemy aliens, those who cannot be identified as such unless they say, "I am German," suffer less. With yellow skin, dark eyes, small stature, and quick movements, we Japanese can be identified at once. If one is to perform as a fifth columnist, among enemy aliens, Germans and Italians are so much better blessed.

February 3

If we vacate two rooms upstairs we use for bedrooms and add a kitchen, we can use it for those who are seeking refuge. It is a time when everyone is having problems, and the thought came to me to offer this.

The governor of California announced that it has been generally decided to first of all, declare eighty-six areas as forbidden districts, and other Japanese would be relocated to other areas. However, assemblymen are clamoring that Washington is saying all Japanese would be relocated to barren areas inland and make them develop it.

We decided to use one of the classrooms downstairs where we had stored all the desks, since school was closed as our bedroom. Therefore, to dispose of the desks, we called the company where we had purchased them and negotiated. Then a Jewish man of about sixty came and said, "For all of them, $11.50."

Since he knows we are desperate, that's it. Further, he says he will not buy the small desks or the blackboards. When we bought them, it was over $250. This is one twentieth the cost; but under the circumstances, it can't be helped. My husband said, "In that case, I will give you all the small desks."

The old man was happy and shook hands. Around fifty desks were hauled away. Knowing that Japanese-language schools are closed forever, I have no regrets. We stored dictionaries and other books we wanted to take with us when we return to Japan in a trunk.

Photographs of the tragedy at Pearl Harbor are starting to come out in the English-language newspapers. Pictures of large battleships turned upside down are terrible! They say it will take about five years to repair the harbor to what it was.

February 6

Today there was a theory that people living in Los Angeles would not be relocated, so everyone is feeling relieved. However, it is difficult to predict how things might change again tomorrow. From Monday, the term *Standard Time* will be changed to *Wartime Time*.

Last night, from eleven fifty-seven until five after midnight, there was a blackout. That was soon after we went to bed, so we knew nothing about it. They say it was because a suspicious airplane was flying around.

In San Francisco, Murakami first name unknown, who was imprisoned for having a shortwave radio and camera, feared being sent to Montana and tried to commit suicide by cutting his wrist and throat with a safety razor but was unsuccessful.

February 7

Pink peach blossom is starting to bloom. Pretty birds of spring are also chirping. The weather is like April in spring in Japan. Here, about the time of the Girl's Festival of March 3, peaches are ripe. Around today we should be past beginning of spring; but because of the war, Japanese calendars are not available, so it is hard to tell.

In Northern California, commuting to work is allowed, but orders came out not to go over five miles, so business people are unexpectedly affected. It seems the number of desperate Japanese households increase daily. The radio announces American victories daily. However, on sea and on the ground, with soldiers with no experience in war, it's not possible to win so easily, and the Japanese give a wry smile.

February 9

Today there will be an important special announcement—impatiently waiting. It was that those living in the aforementioned eighty-six restricted areas depending on area had to voluntarily leave by midnight of the fifteenth or twenty-fourth. Those who did not by those time limits would be arrested. Everyone had thought the government would bear all expenses and assist in moving us to somewhere, but now they are saying move yourselves to an unrestricted area, and those who wanted to discuss it can go to area evacuation consultation centers.

So you move to an unrestricted area. What if that place is also added to the restricted areas at a later date? Undoubtedly, there will be some unlucky ones who will meet that fate. The Japanese are saying, "If we are moved inland, you will get the same food as prisoners of war, so eat delicious food now while you can." Tonight we had no guests, but our family made sukiyaki and ate a lot.

February 10

Afternoon, in the blue sky, I saw a kite made of light black paper way up in the sky. There must be a drawing of a flame thrower on the paper. Nowadays, because of the war, the children's paper kites have drawings of bombers and tanks and battleships, etc.

The English-language newspaper reported that communications with Singapore has been lost—that Japanese Forces are winning and must have occupied the radio station.

Today, in Japan, it is National Foundation Day. Americans too were saying Japan would probably take Singapore by this date, and it has come true. They must be celebrating. In regard to that, it also means that the day of air raids here have come closer. We must be prepared to die. We Japanese are living scattered among Americans like this, so in the event of Japanese air raids, it is not possible to bomb to avoid killing Japanese, so we may die. In other words, it is dying by friendly fire.

Everything is fate. To become a father, a mother, parents and becoming a child and coming into this fleeting world with a life span of so many years may be a thankful trial. It is until we discard the activities of this temporary world and attain eternal life. But once we are born into this life of the world of people, we must cherish our life until the last moment. From now, under whatever circumstances, our family becomes separated; if we are alive when peace comes for about ten days, we will stand in front of City Hall, and we will search for each other; thus, our family of four discussed. Sachiko was listening with eyes full of tears, and she finally started to sob.

February 11

Last night in San Diego, a suspicious airplane came, and there was a blackout for four hours. In the English-language newspaper, it is saying Singapore can probably hold out until this afternoon. The U.S. government, when it designated enemy alien evacuation in order to designate military factories, oil tanks, aqueducts, and other important areas, blacked out those areas in black and published it in newspapers— on a large scale. There are those who said, "If you do this kind of thing, the enemy will know right away. That is a blunder like assisting spies."

So that got my attention, and I thought, *Really, if it was Japan, they would never do a thing like this.*

This must be an example of the American characteristic of being easygoing, generous, and not worrying about small details.

February 13

This morning was foggy, and the roofs of houses are glistening indistinctly. It is cold as if the coldest season of the year has returned. Since New Year, they say the small amount of rainfall is unprecedented. Everywhere is completely dry, and there isn't a day one does not hear the siren of fire trucks. The air is also dry, and from time to time, my throat hurts.

The English-language newspaper is clamoring that enemy aliens will be sent inland, that they won't be sent inland. Farmers who have been ordered to evacuate have to dispose of household goods, farming implements, plow horses, planted fields, and are at wit's end. This becomes a chance for opportunistic white men, and they say each family is losing a couple of thousand of dollars on the average.

Today it seems the British Navy suffered losses by the German Navy, and Churchill was severely criticized in parliament. Americans are good natured and easygoing, and it seems they are always being taken advantage of by the British.

February 18

It became Wartime Time, so time was moved up one hour, and we were forced to get up early. On foggy days, it is still dimly dark out, so I feel uneasy when Yoko goes to school which is some distance away.

The New York English-language newspaper is saying, "The actual losses at Pearl Harbor should be announced. It is not something that can be covered up."

The president says, "There are those who are spreading rumors that we suffered great losses at Pearl Harbor. Don't believe it."

What is this about?

It seems the decision to forcefully moving us Japanese inland had not yet been decided by the Central Government, so in each area, committee members have been selected to gather public opinion. So until March 16, when all those reports are gathered, they say we can definitely remain.

Silk has stopped coming from Japan, so women's stockings have become nylon or cotton, but it seems there were some silk stockings still in the market. However, they say it is from 30 to 40 percent more expensive than pre-war prices. It seems that from the seventy-five colors of women's stockings existing up to now, it has been decided to make it uniform in only four colors.

February 20

The president announced that the defense of the coast has been delegated to chief of the army. They say that tomorrow, they will have a meeting at the White House to discuss evacuating Japanese without waiting for survey results; and if they decide to do so, it will probably take place around March 15.

Earl Warren, the attorney general of California, said that Governor Olson had declared operating licenses to enemy alien doctors, dentists, barbers, real estate brokers, etc., would be denied, but that was illegal. Those licenses would be approved for those who are not specifically declared to be enemy aliens. Government officials are openly discussing differences of opinions, so we become even more confused.

I heard that today, at the Long Beach City Market, every last vegetable/fruit stand and florist shop, all Issei and Nisei, a total of 268 were forced to leave. It is unbearably regrettable that the foundation and places of business the Japanese had built up since the previous great war in Europe through steady hard work was destroyed without a trace by a piece of paper.

February 23

The *Examiner* newspaper reported that Army General Hugh S. Johnson had said, "The U.S. government is saying that the government will not come up with the money but will make the people come up with it. However, under the circumstances, we can't chase him out, so there is nothing to do but bear with it."

If this was in Japan, in time of war, criticizing the government of those in power would probably not be allowed, and newspapers would definitely not publish it—I thought that's how the situation differs in the countries.

Off the cost of Santa Barbara, a submarine appeared, and a suspicious airplane is flying around, so the radio was off for a while. Japanese forces must have come into the coastal sea.

Today I had a big laugh when I heard that in Long Beach when a Japanese was being questioned was asked, *"What is your name?"* he replied, *"Electric Stove."*

This was in the English-language newspaper, and Americans are angry or hooting. "Electric Stove?"

Within the FBI, there are missionaries who spent time in Japan and are very good in Japanese, so saying something like that is not going to fool them. However, when I think of the Japanese feeling of being reluctant in using one's name coming out suddenly at a time like this it was funny, but I also felt sad, and a solemn feeling came over me; and after I laughed, sad tears moistened my eyes.

February 24

The special edition of the newspaper reported that last night, the submarine that showed up off the coast of Santa Barbara, aiming for the oil well towers, fired twenty-five rounds of canon fire, and one round hit and caused $500 worth of damages.

Soon, evacuation inland should be announced. Across the mountain which can be seen to the north where snow is falling, at a place near Bakersfield, they say a camp with barracks is being built, so we may be confined there.

February 25

It is windy, and the doors and windows rattle with high-pitched sounds. It is two forty in the morning. I leaped out of bed at the high-low wavelike sound the air raid siren and turned off the twenty-five-watt night-lights in the upstairs hallway and bathroom. After about fifteen minutes, there was someone pounding loudly on the door of the Mexican neighbor's house to our left. After a while, it seemed like someone half asleep came to answer. A policeman had come and was shouting, "It's blackout! Turn off your light!"

That excited voice was carried on the wind and could be heard from a long distance. The sound of the storm and the roar of an airplane are mixed with a booming sound and induce an eerie feeling. From an adjoining bed, my husband, in a low voice, said, "The boom, boom sounds like canon fire."

"Yes. I wonder if the Japanese Navy is firing canons from the sea again."

The children had awakened and were frightened. They asked, "Father. Mother. Has a war reached the mainland?"

"I wonder!"

Both are frightened and shivering with blankets over their heads.

Morning came, and until the all-clear siren sounded at seven nineteen, I felt uneasy worrying about a rain of bombs coming down on us. In the morning, the first streetcar started moving after the all-clear had sounded, and both the streetcar and bus were crowded with commuters. If you live in America, a sight like this is unusual, and I thought of the overcrowded streetcars in Tokyo.

February 26

Last night, nothing occurred, and morning came. Secretary of Navy Knox announced that an enemy plane flying over Los Angeles was an error. On the other hand, the Department of the Army is saying an enemy reconnaissance plane definitely came. Both departments are publicly engaged in an absurd argument, and newspapers are clearly writing this is thus, and this must be what makes America, America.

It seems the anti-aircraft rounds fired the night before were produced in the 1930s, and one third failed to explode. In the English-language newspaper, there were photos of these useless duds where they had come down on roads and people's yards.

February 27

In today's *Industrial Daily*, there were the following articles:

> Item: "*During the blackout on early morning of the 25th, in the vicinity of 2nd Street and Santa Monica, there was light leaking from a window, so an air raid warden went up the stairs to warn the occupant when a young lady wearing a thin night gown*

came out and asked, 'Is that the sound of real cannons?' When the warden said yes, she fainted into his arms."

Item: *"Due to the sound of antiaircraft artillery firing, babies in wombs must have been startled, and expectant mothers felt birth pangs, and 14 babies were born."*

Item: *"To comply with the blackout, the official in charge of streetlights tried desperately to turn off the lights but was caught up in slow traffic and could not turn them off. Because of that, in one district, streetlights were turned off by shooting them with pistols. Also, there were many who had neon signs on. Mayor asked for everyone's cooperation."*

Item: *"In San Diego, there is a shortage of men for street car operators, and they are hiring women. If the war is prolonged, the emergence of women into the workplace will become remarkable."*

March 2

The moon is bright, and it is like daylight, so thinking it was daylight, I got up, and it was still a little after three. There is no cloud, so flying airplanes can be seen clearly. They say this Wednesday there will be an announcement of mass evacuation, First Stage Seattle area, Second Stage San Francisco area, Third Stage Southern California. Especially in Southern California and neighborhood, they have most of the Japanese, so it will be troublesome and will take time.

March 6

As one of the preparations for the move inland, I have total dentures, and it became loose, so I went to Dr. Yoshida's dental clinic. A person in the waiting room said to me, "We don't know whether this movement inland will take place. It seems Japan has announced that if Japanese are forcefully relocated, prisoners of war will be put to hard labor on road construction. Batavia (Indonesia?) has fallen, and there Japan took three to four thousand prisoners. It seems among them there were many soldiers from Southern California. The parents and siblings of these prisoners don't want to see them put to hard labor in Japan and are sure to protest. The government will hesitate to put out evacuation orders."

Since the war started, Japan's radio seems as if it is one of the means of being saved. We have not been able to directly hear shortwave radio broadcasts since becoming enemy aliens, but we can get news from Americans.

March 7

It is now three months since war broke out. It seems as if ten years and more have passed. I have come to understand too well the saying that suffering makes time seem longer. My husband painted all the trunks; I tidied up my sewing patterns.

Every hour, every second, evacuating inland does not leave my mind for an instant. If evacuating inland was only for enemy aliens, it was understandable; but even if they are ethnically Japanese, about half are American citizens. I could understand if they said children must go with their parents. There are many of age who from the time of their birth were completely raised as Americans and only can only speak broken Japanese.

To treat all alike has confused many. It seems there are those who have lost hope, become self-destructive, or frustrated. Have Americans in power given sufficient thought to this matter?

Another thing is the communists. Since the war, they have been running wild and like a bug in a lion have caused considerable suffering to the Japanese. Maybe they thought that their comrades would be excluded, but no such a thing happened. The little wheel of cause and effect, reaping what you sow came around so fast.

They say the exchange of diplomats has been agreed to, but Ambassador Nomura said, "I will stay and suffer alongside my countrymen. I definitely do not intend to return alone." Even if it is a rumor, it gladdens me.

March 9

It is the time of year when tree leaves are pretty. But for those of us where are future is pitch black, we do not have the presence of mind to enjoy it. Because it is war, even if losing your base, your position, your fortune, losing it all is to be expected, to have the four of us in our family separated, and to be erased off the face of the earth by Japanese bombs or American bullets—and if that happens, should we resent Japan, or should we resent America? Japanese in America who are facing this danger in front of us, isn't this an unheard of and never-to-occur-again strange circumstances?

There is a story going around that the expected location to where we will be relocated will be Owens Valley or another candidate is Parker Dam in Arizona, and near each is a power station; and if Japan bombs the water source, we will be situated in depressed areas, and all Japanese will die, and that is why Japan will not bomb these sites—that is what Americans are thinking. Can that be true? Or is it just rumor?

March 11

People who want me to sew them clothes and slacks come. I turn them all down, but for those who insist, I drafted them a pattern. In the paper, it says when we go to Owens Valley, they will set up a factory, and those who can operate motor machines will be offered jobs, and the pay will be the same as those working in war industry factories.

Mrs. Mitsudo and I had been planning to invite five or six others and setting up a sewing center and making various work clothes with a volume sales small profit margin principle, but Mrs. Mitsudo, upon seeing the paper, said, "We all know how to operate machines, so let's become women factory workers. That way, we can make $18–$20 a week."

Fine! Women factory workers. That sounds amusing. Teacher, wife of a church minister, newspaper writer, and now factory worker—many occupations have come into my life. However, if I become a factory worker, it will be eight hours of work each day. Therefore, the primary problem will be whether my health continues or not. To fall and perish—I also had a pathetic feeling.

My husband will think of something and work too. If I can make about $80 a month, during the duration of the war, our family of four will not go hungry. During peacetime, things one never dreamed of and surprising things occur. Rolled that way, pushed this way, this life as an enemy national too—if I can live through this, it will not only become the most valuable experience in my lifetime. It will become something people of both Japan and America will want to know.

Until this war, I loved Japan, and I also love America just as much, so I feel like I am between a rock and a hard place, and my distress is even greater.

March 13

Ah, the fateful day has finally arrived. Today my husband was arrested. It is sad if I think this might be our final parting. It is as if I am being wedged into a dark, dark place underground. It was close to twelve.

When I came home from going out, my husband came rushing out of the reception room and said, "Me or you, and maybe the both of us, but soon they will be here to take us in. Right now, Mr. Onodera called and said all the *nishihonganji* (Buddhist temple) ministers, with exception of Minister Mori and Minister Ishiura, have been taken. With Zenshuji, with exception of Supervisor Etchi, even Mrs. Suzuki has been taken, and then our mom was taken. They had about ten papers with names of those to be taken written on it. They will probably come to our place soon. He said to hurry and be ready. We have to put all our valuables in one trunk. The FBI probably won't be here until one, so let's hurry and eat."

All the blood in my body drained, and I turned pale. Going through the motion, I ate one bowl of rice with tea poured over it. After that, I gathered all the sewing drawings and patterns I had learned up to now, sewing books from Hawaii, and the U.S. and other records I thought important. While my husband was packing those in the trunk, I turned on the washing machine. After I am gone, I wanted to make our young small children's load even a bit lighter.

They say they are going to do away with all Japanese-language school teachers.

Three thirty in the afternoon, a large peony-colored car stopped at our house. Three large white men quickly got off and came treading up the steps. *They've finally come*, I thought. They rang the doorbell, so I went out. One in a shouting manner said, "Is Tokumon Aoki here? We are the FBI. Is this your house?"

I instantly saw that the two who came earlier were gentlemanly, but these were different.

"Yes. My husband is here. Please come in."

I thought I was speaking as calmly as I could without getting excited, but my voice was high pitched and hoarse. The three FBI agents came hurriedly in and went right to the bookshelves. They went to the bookshelves in the two rooms and pulled them all out and examined them. They said, "Bring out all your textbooks."

I went to another shelf and brought out two bundles of textbooks. Then the agent that seemed to understand Japanese jerked out about twenty books. He then went back to the bookshelf and began to pull out select books. Looking at them, they were mostly children's stories, and among them was *Children Who Come to the Red Soil,* which I received from Ogawa Sueaki Sensei at the end of the year before last. Fortunately, my book, *Shadow of the Heart,* was not taken. But most regrettable was the scrapbook with cloth cover about two inches which contained my essays, commentaries, children's stories in Japanese I had written when in Hawaii for the *Japan Hawaii Times* and *Hawaii News* was taken.

One of the FBI agents said to my husband, "Prepare some warm clothing."

So I added a leather briefcase, handkerchief, soap, Band-Aid, and some other miscellaneous items to the previously prepared suitcase. My husband opened his wallet and looked and said to me in Japanese, "I don't need this much money, so you hold this much." And he took out $60 in front of me.

When I said, "I don't need it, so you take it with you," and tried to push it back, the FBI agent who seemed to understand Japanese said, "You should accept the money."

Even then, my husband carried $85. To Yoko and Sachiko who were sobbing, my husband said, "Take care of your health and listen to your mother." And then he said to me, "All of you, take care of your health. Because if we are alive, we will meet again."

Then to Mrs. A and Mrs. Y who saw him off, he said, "Please take care of things."

From his lapel button hole was hung a baggage tag with his name and a number. He was now transformed into a walking baggage. We saw him off up to the front road where he was placed in the car. The car carrying my husband who looked intently at the children started to move without emotion. Ah, he is gone! I was at a loss and suddenly started to feel I was wandering in a vast desolate place. The two children sat together on the first step of the wide cement steps in front of the house and in the cold evening wind, sobbed forever.

While I was adding those few items to my husband's suitcase, Yoko was being asked many questions by one of the FBI agents. After my husband had been taken, she said, "The FBI is really hateful. He said the reason we are being treated like this is penalty for Japan making a sneak attack on Pearl Harbor."

So that was it. However, the FBI agent and you are both American citizens. To say you have the blood of the enemy and only for that reason to blame you doesn't make sense. Those words are for Japanese like your father and your mother. However, for your father and for your mother, nothing can be done about this hardship except to accept it as penance for sins in a prior life.

Oh, Yoko! Oh, Sachiko! Please forgive us. You are too young to know how to resolve these sufferings through religion. However, if you live through this and when you become adults, and when you begin to become aware of the beauty, the intelligence, the mental depth of the essence of the spirituality of the Far East you were born with, then you will probably not regret having been born a Japanese American or having been given life by your father and mother.

After a while, a number of neighbors came by to console us. They say Mr. Nozaki and Pres. Kashu Maichi Fujii (California Japanese daily news) and over two hundred others who had been confined at Tujunga camp were transferred last night to the confinement center in New Mexico. And as the next step, from last night Japanese-language teachers and business people, some four hundred fifty were taken in. Among Japanese-language teachers, there must be some women. I must have been among those who should have been taken, but it seems if both parents are teachers and there are two or more children under the age of twelve, the mother will not be taken.

Sachiko had asked the FBI, "If you take my mother, we are young and can't do anything. Are you really going to come for my mother?"

The FBI agent had replied, "We are not going to take your mother, so don't worry."

"No matter how long we cry, it is not going to help. So let's go think about what we will take to Father when we go to see him."

With the two children, we wrote items we would take on the blackboard in the reception room.

On Wall Street, they had a wager on the war ending this August, and those who bet it would end outnumbered the other by ten to one. They say the policy is that while the war continues, stock prices will be allowed to rise, but Americans hate to see their soldiers killed, so it must be a reflection of their feeling that even if it's necessary to throw away the money, buying peace is desirable. And in American now, they are saying we must buckle down because its costs $85,000 to kill one enemy soldier.

March 14

I did not sleep a wink, and daybreak came. It is raining. It is a spiteful chilling rain, and around ten, even the wind joined in. I went to the California bank to change my husband's savings account over to the children's account. In the afternoon, my younger sister came with her child to express her condolences. I received a chicken last night from one of the callers, so we fried that and we had dinner together. In a disappointed voice, Sachiko said, "Father's not here."

Today I was busy arranging the goods to take to my husband and fixing the sleeve of the woolen fabric shirt I had bought the other day.

It seems visiting hours at the confinement center is on Sundays from one to three, but my husband had said, "Don't come to visit." And he did not write to inform us about visiting hours. But tomorrow, I arranged to have Mr. I's son bring out his car. With the children, I put various items in a large *shingen* (duffel) bag. With a suitcase, even when empty, one has to carry it. I thought with a *shingen* bag, it is convenient because when empty, you can lightly fold it and put it away in your suitcase. I selected a woolen fabric one with six large rivets on the bottom.

To investigate educators and religious leaders who are always teaching others to be good, I wonder what is happening. I have no idea what the communists have been informing, but if they investigate thoroughly, there probably isn't a single one that performed as a spy. It pains me to think how my husband might be doing in a camp like that on a bone-chilling day like this.

As I write, I am drowsy. Perhaps I can sleep tonight.

March 15

From morning, it is clear, and the sky is beautiful. Our hearts, however, conversely, gets darker and darker. From morning, I purchased things in the neighborhood to take to my husband. Then I added it to the *shingen* bag of last evening. Doing this and that, it became twelve o'clock.

As agreed upon, Mr. I's son, bringing his little sister along, brought his car, so I carried the bags with the items to take; and with my two daughters, I got into the car. The son knew the way, so it didn't take thirty minutes to get to the Tujunga camp. We parked the car in the rear, and as we got out, we could see those being investigated standing around in the promenade. They all looked depressed as if they had all agreed to do so.

Sachiko spotted her father and shouted, "Oh, there's Father wearing a brown coat!"

Indeed, you could tell it is him. However, it is about seven yards away; and sadly, we cannot get any closer. It looked like he had spotted us and took out his handkerchief and waved it. We raised our hands and waved. Also, Mr. S and Mr. M—they are fellow school teachers and church related people—they are all familiar faces. We went around to the front and arranged a visitation. Our name starts with *A*, so we stood in front of a desk that said A–I. Fortunately, we were first; and when one o'clock came, we were called. However, we were told, "Only one guard speaks Japanese, so unless you are assigned to that guard. You must speak English."

My husband was the first to be called ahead of everyone. By unexpected good luck, our guard was a Korean who spoke Japanese. My husband thought we would not come to see him, but in preparation in case we did, he had written over a page of things on twenty-four-line manuscript paper which he hurriedly started to read:

"Underwear to include summer wear, slipper and shoes to add leather soles, eyeglasses, clothes, belts are necessary. To stress that I am to insist, I must remain for the welfare of the children if the FBI comes for me. Put checking and savings accounts in order. To send Hakuin Zenshi's two books, *Yasenkanwa* and *Orategama,* and other things."

I reported on what we had brought today, and about being asked to make a recommendation about Mr. G's wedding by Mrs. A. And about disposition of bureaus and book cases, relocation destination, insurance money, bank safety box, and other things.

My husband held the finger tips that the children had extended through the opening in the wire mesh and said, "Take care of your health, and listen to your mother."

The children started to cry. I too cried. The guard said, "That should be enough."

Lastly, my husband said to Mr. I's son, "Thank you very much. Please give my regards to your father and mother."

They say visitations are limited to three minutes, but we didn't put on any time limit and talked without a pause for about seven minutes.

Returning, I was discouraged. At Mr. I's residence, I went in and thanked them; and when I returned home, there were many visitors offering condolences. From then until evening, we had visitors, and among them was one I did not know. He said, "For six years, every day without fail, I read your essays and commentaries with great interest. I am Mr. M from Pasadena, and Sugimachi Sensei and his wife were both taken with only what they had on leaving their fifteen-year-old daughter by herself. I understand you have two daughters and wondered what had happened. I was worried you both might have been taken and came to see."

In the evening, Mrs. M came to discuss moving, so I went to talk to Reporter Itami who lived next door. I was told, "Rather than the matter of moving, you are in danger. No matter how many babies there are, under the law, there is no human feeling or anything. There are seven, eight families where both parents were taken. The way it's going, in the next arrests, you will probably definitely be taken. Please be prepared for that."

So that's how it is. I felt as if everything in front was pitch-dark. When I steadied my shaking steps and went home, I had people who had come to my place to discuss evacuation gather in the reception room and asked them to first look after my children and then my baggage. Among them, to Mr. G, I told him about the money the children were carrying, about the most precious thing in my baggage, looking after the children at the destination site, and things in detail and had him acknowledged that.

I may only have four or five more days of freedom. After this, my husband will be sent to a confinement center in New Mexico, the children to an unknown inland location, and we are going to be separated. We do not know if we will ever meet again. I had my neighbor Mr. Itami promise to explain the circumstances and plead my case to the priest at Maryknoll as my last thread of hope should I be taken.

However, everything has come to where it has come. It is no use to struggle now. All is left to fate. Now that I clearly understand my circumstances, even though I am hungry, I cannot eat. Morning, one cup of coffee, one banana, no lunch. At lunchtime, visitors came continuously, and I had no time to eat. And for dinner, one bowl of soup. Therefore, if the wind is a little bit strong, I feel as if I will be blown away.

March 16

About dawn, I thought I dozed for just a moment, but I saw a dream. At one of the rooms of the Los Angeles Nishihonganji Church, those who were confined were being allowed visitors. The visitors are sitting on brown silk cushions on tatami, which really doesn't exist at that church. Then a white policeman grabs a detainee and brings him to the visitor. When it became my husband's turn, and just when he sat down on a kerosene box, I awoke. There were many things I wanted to talk about, so it was regrettable.

The Japanese-language teachers, businessmen, religious leaders who were taken in from Thursday to Sunday of last week will be allowed their last visitations on Wednesday, the day after tomorrow; and on Thursday, they will be sent to confinement center in New Mexico or Montana. Then they say, from Thursday night, more will be taken in—I heard that kind of rumor. Therefore, on Monday, Tuesday, Wednesday—those three days—I will first get the items ready to take to my husband; and second, I will prepare for being taken in myself. I cannot expect my children to bring me anything; I will be careful not to forget anything. Third, I will prepare as much as I can for the children's evacuation inland.

After breakfast and sending the children off to school, I thought of how to save the most important things I did not want to lose—that would be the clippings of my essays and children's stories I wrote for the *Kashu Mainichi* newspaper for eight years. The next would be five volumes of sewing pattern drawings, four or five different rulers, three or four hundred dress patterns I designed, and then about twenty volumes of sewing books and others. The authorities will probably not confiscate the sewing items, but when they were here before and checked the bookcase, they took all my writings during the time I was in Hawaii; and when I think of that, it's definite they will take these clippings of articles. It was known the writing was plain like a meal of rice, but strangely, readers followed it. Essays and clippings up to now had been stored in trunk. I took those out and put into a pillow case and tied it with a string and asked Ms. M to store it with her baggage.

Then I went down town and shopped for one or two things, dropped by Mrs. SM's sewing place, and arranged my sewing things I had kept there when I got a phone call from Mrs. A., who I had asked to watch my house.

"Hurry and come home. They came."

"The FBI?"

"Yes."

That's what it was. Mrs. A must have worried about shocking me. She did not blurt out the FBI had come. Even then, that was fast. I carried my sewing implements and hurried home. It was five minutes before twelve. Mrs. A told me, "It was around 11:00 a.m. Two westerners came and said Hisa Aoki, Hisa Aoki, many times, and asked if the person was here, so I replied you had gone to take care of some matters in town. They looked very unsatisfied. They asked when you would return, so I said probably around 2:00 p.m. They then went home. I called around to likely places you may have gone."

So I have two more hours. I will do as much as I can. During that time, Mrs. Y prepared lunch for me and said, "Your lunch is ready." But I just couldn't eat. I only had half a banana and a cup of coffee for breakfast, and I am hungry, but I am choked up, and I don't want to eat. However, it would be embarrassing to pass out, so I cracked open a raw egg and closed my eyes and gulped it down.

I called Mr. G and asked him to get time off and come right away. There were things I wanted to ask him to take care of after I am gone, and I wanted him to interpret for me. He immediately came driving his car. Just at this time Mrs. K, a parent of one of the Japanese-language students came to console me on my husband being taken, so I hurriedly explained the situation to her and asked her to bring Sachiko home from school. Then I hurriedly packed.

Two o'clock came and went; two thirty also went. Three o'clock came. The FBI did not come. Mr. G is a manager of a market, so just knowing whether he is there or not, there has a big impact it is worrisome. I can't just have him waiting idly by forever, so I decided to ask him to return to his store as soon as Yoko returns after three. Sachiko came home, and when she learned what was going on, she cried. Yoko came home. It happened just as Mr. G opened the door to go out. They're here!

There was no mistake it was the FBI. It was one man. This official was not like the men who had taken my husband and was soft-spoken and seemed like a completely relaxed type of personality. It seemed the FBI agent thought Mr. G was Hisa Aoki. Mr. G explained, "No, I am this person's friend." Mr. G had managed a store catering to White customers for eight years and seemed to know instantly how to handle this man.

After leading him to the reception room, he politely asked the FBI agent, "Please have a seat."

The FBI agent, upon learning I was Hisa Aoki, bluntly asked, "Are you a teacher at the Hollywood Japanese Language School?"

"Yes, I am."

At this, this must be an investigation from the Hollywood Language School. I had been teaching at that school only one day a week on Saturdays. The head of the school had not yet been taken, so I immediately realized that. Then he asked about various things for about fifty minutes, about my husband, about the children, about before I got married, the date I came to the United States, the date I returned to visit Japan, how long I stayed, relatives, remittances to Japan, and completely filled three note pages. When I am talking in Japanese, he does not write. That must mean he does not seem to understand Japanese.

Finally, Mr. G pointed at the sobbing children behind me and asked, "The father of these children were taken Friday, and now if you take their mother, there is no one to look after them. Then they won't even be able to evacuate inland. Isn't whether these small children are treated well or badly under these circumstances your responsibility?"

The FBI agent agreed and asked, "Is there a phone?" He stood in front of the phone and explained the circumstances to Public Prosecutor Palmer and asked what he should do about the mother. He used extremely respectful language. Public Prosecutor Palmer appeared to have replied, "Leave it as it is and let her look after the children."

The FBI agent said, "In that case, fine. You can stay to look after the children and will not be taken."

"Thank you," Mr. G said and expressed his appreciation. The children jumped up and shouted, "Oh, oh . . ." I was set free. I can stay with the children. Rolling waves of tears wet my hands, my skirt, and even my shoes.

March 17

In this morning's *Industrial Daily,* it said the governors of six coastal states had been invited by the government to discuss preparation for the confinement and internment of ethnic Japanese. It said that was because Senator Stevens who heads the Senate subcommittee of immigration is to present the plan to the senate next week. It said the reason for the plan is:

> "The present law providing citizenship to Japanese Americans was the result of the Supreme Court decision forty-five years ago giving citizenship to Chinese who were born in the United States, and complying with that, Japanese born in the United States were given citizenship. My proposed amendment of today's main point is the confinement of Japanese Americans. The reason is because Japan considers all descendants of Japanese to be citizens of the Japanese Emperor."

> (This is not true. After 1924, any child born of a Japanese father not registered with the Japanese embassy/consulate within two weeks was denied Japanese citizenship.)

Whether this passes or not is a separate issue; to have such a proposal presented leaves one speechless.

For about two hours, I went to a quiet room where no one else was present and thought deeply about what will happen from now. Above all, I must not let my body deteriorate any further. I must live like I am one step away from dying. I must make an effort to eat a lot and must not let my body wear away from exhaustion. Then I must work in moderation.

After going inland, I will work at sewing or something. Then my children and I, the three of us, will be able to eat. What will happen will happen. It is sad, it is regrettable, it is pitiful. I was deep in an indescribable feeling for a long while. I must be out of tears, and today I hardly cried at all.

March 18

It is the last visitation day for my husband. I had Sachiko excused from school and am taking her with me to visit father, but Yoko's school is very strict, and it would be difficult for her to be excused to go just to visit. And another thing, Mr. G is taking us and his car is a two-seater; and although three can somehow manage to get in, four cannot, so I let her go to school.

I had Sachiko write a letter in English, and I wrote one in Japanese, but to make sure it would not be taken by guards, I checked it three times. Leaving it unsealed, I put it into the suitcase side pocket. There were items from friends, and it became a large luggage. Mr. G returned at noon, so I prepared sandwiches and boiled eggs we could eat on the way. We got lost a few times but even then arrived at the Tujunga Confinement Center a little after one o'clock.

We registered as visitors and were allowed to meet with a wire screen between us but only for two minutes. My husband was wearing a dark blue double-button coat—his better one—and he was wearing glasses. He said, "I am doing Nishi-style physical exercise, so do not worry about my health."

We both read what we had written, but without fully understanding each other, we ran out of time. In parting, my husband thanked Mr. G and grasped Sachiko's fingers twice. Tomorrow night, he will be sent to faraway New Mexico, and I wonder how long before we will be able to meet again.

At night, I went to bed and thought I finally fell asleep when the doorbell rang repeatedly. It is five minutes to midnight. I got up and looked through the window, and it was someone I knew—Ms. S, a seamstress of twenty-five or twenty-six, standing there. I thought it was strange and opened the door.

She said, "By eight in the morning, we have to find one thousand single persons to send to Owens Valley and must run around all night. The order came out at five this evening, and unless we send one thousand men by eight in the morning, this Los Angeles may face the same fate as Terminal Island. If we are told to get out with only what we are wearing within forty-eight hours, it will be terrible, so we divided the work among us, and I am sorry to bother you in the middle of the night, but I came to ask if there is anyone in your household who can go."

The situation is urgent.

March 20

I awoke. It is five thirty. When I think how I will handle all this baggage, I cannot sleep. Around ten o'clock, Mrs. T, a parent of a student, made a condolence visit. She told me those confined at Tujunga will stay there until around next Monday. After she went home, I went to the California Bank and made safety deposit box advance payment for two years. If the war is not over by March 3, 1944, I can send rental fees by check. Then I had my safety deposit box opened. After my husband was taken, it was frozen, but I had been authorized to open it for living necessities, but each item I removed was inspected.

After ten o'clock at night, student-parent Mr. Ishimoto brought vegetables. And he said, "Let's move during next week. Please hurry preparing."

Taking seventeen families, Mr. Ishimoto is going to voluntarily evacuate one hundred fifty miles inland and from the other day had me to join them. I feel faint. At the same time, I feel a coldness in the core of my being and cannot sleep.

March 21

All day I was very busy arranging my baggage and completely fatigued. I had the children assisted in tying a number of woven containers with ropes. Even if my husband is taken, if I had a son, it would be so helpful when work requiring strength was involved. The boys in Japan—even if the second son was sickly—the oldest was strong. When I thought that, I again felt sad.

I received a call from Mrs. Nozaki saying she received a letter from her husband. He wrote that the camp in New Mexico has many vacant rooms. He is happy when someone he knows comes, but he feels sorry for them, so he prays they will be people he does not know. It is cold, and the mountains in the vicinity are white with snow and things like that.

It is rumored that relocation to inland Owens Valley will be by the army, so it is safe, but relocating on your own can be dangerous; but for some reason, I do not want to go to Owens Valley. When I told Yoko, "Relocating will be soon, so quit school and help me," she said, "Please let me attend until the day before we move." Sachiko didn't want to but said, "In that case, I will make arrangements to quit on Monday." Both are assistant class leaders, so they must hate to leave.

Two or three days ago, Reporter Itami said, "As a leader of Kibei Nisei, I am being watched by the authorities, so I can't just sit around. Next Monday, I will join the advance party and go to Owens Valley. Also, all the employees are going inland, so *Kamai* (the *Kashu Mainichi* newspaper) will cease publication this week."

It stopped as of today. In looking back, fifteen years ago, Mr. Fujii Sei, to provide guidance and protest the rights of Japanese in America, invested his own money and published the *Kashu Mainichi* newspaper; and during that time, he left many glorious deeds. When I think I too was privileged to write for the newspaper for about eight years, I am overcome with a lonely feeling.

March 23

It is helpful that Sachiko took leave from school and is assisting. Of three large rugs I had, I was thinking of taking one with me to camp and sell the other two when the wife of the owner of an apartment nearby came over and asked to see the rugs. Then as if it was an order, she said she would buy one for $6 and one for $5. I thought it was a little better than selling to a scrap dealer, so I agreed. It was less than one twelfth of five years ago.

Mr. Ishimoto said he had found an area to relocate to in Colorado, so now he is saying we should go there. It is much more convenient than the earlier location; the children's school is half a mile away, and the post office is a mile and a half. At this time, any place will do.

March 24

The sun is warm, the wisteria is almost blooming, and the long wall area is bright where it is wrapped around. From morning, all day long I packed items and wrote identification and was busy, and my back and arms ached. Yoko had asked to attend school until the day before evacuating, but she worried about the urgent situation, and today she quit school and returned.

The word that the Japanese were having forced sales of household goods had gone around, and they came one after another asking if we had anything to sell. Today a bald-headed, dumpy Jewish man came and asked if we would sell our refrigerator for a hundred dollars. It is a new style Frigidaire, less than two years old. I thought that was an appropriate price, but Yoko said, "No, we will not," and rejected it.

The Maytag wash machine was purchased about nine months ago, and I was very happy with it and prized it dearly and had no intention of selling it from the beginning. A woman of mixed birth came again today. I had turned her down yesterday by clearly saying, "I will not sell this." Again, she says, "Won't you think about it and sell?" She is persistent. She must be attracted to it. It is pure white shining ceramic and had been taken care of, so it is like new. On its square body, it has in bright red in stylish lettering its company name, Maytag. Nothing helps a housewife more than a wash machine.

On top of that, I saw a beautiful fantasy world in the seven colors of soap bubbles and wrote a number of children's stories. Last summer, they said it could be used for thirty years, so I paid $160 and bought it. Now nothing is made other than military items, so they say in half a year, it will be worth twice as much. They say for peacetime production to resume will take two years after the war is over, so during the war, which no one can predict how long it will continue, it will reach an unpredictable price.

Mr. Ishimoto says he will take us to a farm in Colorado, and in my case, I would not have to go into the field by taking care of the children of seventeen families and sewing the clothes of workers, which is enough to guarantee a living; but, after all, I will have to prepare at least $1,600 for the living expense of the three of us. My husband said to sell one or two shares of stock and prepare the money, but he has been taken in, so it can't be sold right away.

My share was frozen when war broke out because I had visited Japan a year ago. I have no choice. I will have to go wherever evacuation site the government decides. My younger sister had at first decided to voluntarily evacuate to Nevada, and when that no longer became possible, she decided to go to Owens Valley.

It seems the majority of those who remain in their homes have decided to go to Owens Valley. A cold feeling comes and is shaking the root of my soul.

March 25

Because of delay in the transfer of detainees at Tujunga camp, it became possible today to again visit my husband. Morning, with Sachiko, the two of us went to the storeroom of the closed store on the front street where we had made arrangements to store part of our baggage and opened our nailed-shut trunk and wooden boxes and looked for the books my husband had asked for, and we found one but couldn't find the other, so I took out two or three others that might be suitable. Then I got a one-piece serge pajama for summer wear, a dress shirt, a work shirt, and a photo of myself and the children, a box of Shogetsu sushi—and bundled it up in a *furoshiki* (cloth used for that purpose). And then I affixed a white cloth and wrote my husband's name on it in English letters.

After 10:00 a.m., we arranged to meet soon after arriving at Tujunga. Today I talked of disposition of household goods, insurance, and of the matter of relocating. When I told my husband, "Unless I put together $1,500, we will be in a humiliating position of being someone's guest, and there is no reason to live like that by tagging along so . . ."

He said, "In that case, it can't be helped, so go where the government tells you."

After that, someone must have brought it to him. He handed Baby Ruths (candy bars) through the metal mesh to the two children. I was glad my husband looked quite healthy. Today it was a Nisei guard, so we were allowed to talk a fairly long time. When we were told "I'm sorry, but time is up" and departed from the metal barrier, Sachiko raised her voice and cried.

On the way home, we stopped at the Maryknoll school, and I met with the priest and asked him about registration for relocating and baggage storage. He said, "Register for relocating on Wednesday. Where to store baggage should be designated by the government, so read the newspaper."

March 26

From tomorrow, this Southern California like Northern California will be declared a restricted area. No matter what, it is a difficult situation. In the evening, younger sister came with Nobuhiro and said, "This place is seven miles from my place, and I will no longer be able to come here, so I came today to say good-bye for a while."

After Sunday, going to another state will not be allowed. I had no connection with Colorado after all. I thought. We are gradually being squeezed. I am exhausted with remorse and sadness, and my body may soon be reduced to skin and bones.

To my husband, I wrote, "From tomorrow, we cannot go outside of five miles, and to get permission requires a tedious application, so I will not visit next Sunday. If you need anything, let me know, and I will send it." However, soon after that, I heard from Mr. O that "in town, there was someone who saw those at Tujunga being sent by four busses to Santa Fe station" and was disappointed. They will probably to be taken to New Mexico. Tears flowed as I thought of not meeting again until the war was over. An infinite sadness like having to roam an ocean alone tightly gripped my chest. The shape of a cloud wandering the cloudy sky also adds to the grief.

March 27

The plan for today is to store valuables at the *nishihonganji*. Putting bars on windows, making double doors, having a night guard, they say they will guard the goods until war's end. There are many people storing goods. Around two in the afternoon, the hauling company truck arrived. We will be hauling a refrigerator, washing machine, sewing machine, metal trunk, medium trunk, one large wooden box, one set of carpenter tools in brass case, one *kohri* (large Japanese bamboo storage case) total eight in all. I went by street car to the *nishihonganji* annex.

After waiting awhile, the baggage arrived. The receptionist and attendants were all people known to me, and they received me warmly. The storage fee was calculated based on the war lasting two years and totaled $19. If these items worth $1,700–$1,800 are returned safely to me at the end of the war, it is cheap. About 70 percent of Japan town is shut down, and it is painful, and one feels a loneliness with a sunken feeling. Today I have lost the energy to even think. Everything around looks dreary, and like a mermaid in a children's story living in a world at the bottom of a deep ocean, I just wanted to stay quietly cowered down.

March 30

It must be something I ate; my stomach aches. It hurt like it is shooting out of my back and shoulders; it comes up toward my breast and throat. It is painful lying down on a bed, so I sat up in bed many times. The children say, "Mother, with you ill, there is nothing we can do with all this baggage, so let's just throw all this away and leave."

My husband and I both loved tools and things, so we had bought a lot of things, so at a time like this, it is a problem. If we sell them it won't amount to much, but even then, there are many items, and it would be a shame to throw them away. Recently, the scrap dealers would buy things they can make a profit on; but knowing what we can't take would just be abandoned, they will not buy most items.

If too much suffering which is too cruel and sadness which is too deep are visited on one person at once, they strangely neutralize each other, and I think it just leaves one in a dazed state.

April 1

In the controlling law announced a few days ago, from after midnight yesterday, there was a clause that Nisei also must turn in shortwave radios, cameras, firearms, explosives, etc., so finally we cannot know for sure what shortwave broadcasts from Japan talked about.

They had said when we are confined in government assembly centers, those who work will receive a minimum of $54 to a maximum of $95 (a month); but from around yesterday, the government is saying they can only pay everyone $21, the same as recruits. When it has come to this, those things don't matter.

April 3

At two in the afternoon, Mr. G and Ms. M, at the home of Mr. G's elder sister's house located nearby, held a simple Buddhist wedding ceremony with a reverend from the Taishi Church officiating. Since the times are the times, groom Mr. G had on a black suit; the bride was wearing a new gray suit. The four best friends were each wearing dark clothes that did not attract attention. Only the officiant was wearing colored clothes and an embroidered surplice (loose outer garment) and stood out.

After the ceremony, Reverend Sogabe said, "Like a needle that sews clothing, the husband must stand up in the world and sharply and bravely pierce his way forward. The wife, like the thread behind the needle, must follow and support her husband. The needle and thread are two different things, but unless they come together as one, it cannot do its function. Today to these two who are starting on a new phase in life, I offer these words as my words of congratulations."

It was short but impressive lecture. Mr. G had gone to Japan while still an infant and had completed one year at Tokyo City Middle School when he returned to the United States, completed grammar school and high school in an amazing short time of three years, graduated from college, and had been working as a manager of a vegetable market for eight years.

My place was not too far from his place of work, and he had been living in an empty room upstairs for about two years. Then war began, and Ms. M had come to rent a room downstairs; and from time to time, the two would meet. Ms. M was tall and slender and a dignified young lady. She had been deeply influenced by her close association with the wife of the head of the Taishi Buddhist Church, and that was evident in the way she spoke and her courteous mannerism, and she would shame no one wherever she went.

Theirs was a fateful bonding. After meeting, things went so smoothly, and in less than a month, they had this happy event.

April 5

Today was the last day for the Rafu Shimpo. It is lonely to see one of the Japanese-language newspapers disappear.

In today's news, it was reported that the International Red Cross investigation had learned the three hundred sixty American soldiers and noncombatants taken prisoner on Wake Island and Guam were at the Zentsuji confinement center on Shikoku and being treated well.

April 7

The weather was clear from morning. Plums had gotten completely large, and looking up at the tree, its round shape brings forth sour juice in your mouth. Last year, *shiso* (beefsteak plant) seed must have spilled; and in the corner of the flower bed, there are many tens of double-leaf purple *shiso* plants thriving in the warm air.

On the Australian front, it is reported that Allied Forces shot down thirty-five or forty Japanese planes. And Allied Forces had three aircraft that failed to return. In the morning paper, it was reported that the city of Darwin has turned into a ghost town; and that, in its victory, British forces had made a planned retreat. To say it made a planned retreat in its victory is just so typical of the way Americans write.

Special correspondent for the *Chicago Sun*, Nick Baker reported that "it seems that Japanese troops sent to Australia are short on rations. The fact that most are not wearing shoes gives us a strange feeling, etc., etc."

April 8

After breakfast—today is the Flower Festival—I realized it was Buddha's birthday; and having some glutinous rice left over, I made some red bean rice and placed an offering at our Buddhist household altar.

Evening, I was again arranging our baggage; and at exactly nine, the air raid sirens sounded, high and low as if crying, and continued for two minutes. We instantly turned off all lights. Fortunately, the children had changed into pajamas, but I did not have time to change, so I crawled into bed just as I was. There is nothing to do in the pitch-dark.

Streetlights too were immediately turned off. Street cars and automobiles also stopped, and in just a short while, it turned into a city of death. Everyone was saying the days to be alert this month are

April 3, 8, and 29, but nothing had happened on April 3. So thinking something may finally happen today, I kept tossing on my bed.

Yoko said, "Mother, there were many airplanes flying around from morning. Among them, I saw a strange large airplane."

I said, "That might have been the B-19." It can carry ninety-six people and is the world's largest. It is said to have been purchased by the navy for $1 million and being tested. Now again, low flying airplanes create a continuous roar that is painful to the ear.

Even then, for a while, I was nodding; and at 11:15 p.m., the all-clear siren which did not undulate high and low sounded. Then the city lighted up, and the sound of street cars and automobiles were heard at once. Did we have enemy planes come, or was it another practice?

April 18

This morning had large headlines that Tokyo was bombed. It says four hundred houses burned, but I wonder what area. Are my sons who are at my elder sister's house in Shiba safe? I am so worried I cannot stand it. What size formation of airplanes was it? American radios do not say from what base for fear of providing information that would benefit the enemy. But they say they will provide details at a later date. Countrymen are excitedly saying it is from a base is in China, no, from Russia, from Manchuria—it must have been from an aircraft carrier.

April 20

There is a famous tarot reading fortune-teller living about a block away to the east from my house. Mrs. A says, "After school today when Yoko comes home, can I borrow her as an interpreter? I want to ask many things . . ."

Our evacuation destination had not been decided, so until it is definite, Yoko had returned to attending school. Since Mrs. A said that, I too decided to go and see.

The fortune-teller was a man of over fifty with dark brown skin, two missing front teeth, and his eyes are round and glaring, but he is smiling and very charming. He is a mix of many generations of black and brown, and my two children who can tell nationality with one glance both said, "We can't tell the nationality of this person."

Mrs. A had her fortune read and left the room, so I sat down. He took out two types of cards and turned them over on their back and said, "Divide them into three stacks." And when I did as instructed, he turned it over to the face side and was looking at it, and then said, "This relocation should be a very fruitful good trip for you."

I asked why. He said, "Because you will be sent to a place better than what you are now thinking."

I told Yoko in Japanese, "Father was a Japanese-language teacher, so he was taken by the FBI and is now in the Santa Fe camp, so ask him when he can come home."

To Yoko's query, the fortune-teller was going through the cards and said, "Your father has not done one thing wrong, so at the latest, he will come back to you at the camp where you are."

Next, I asked, "When will the war end?"

The fortune-teller said as if it was a matter of fact, "Japan wants to end it this year or the next, but America will not end it for three or four years. America will win, and the war will end."

I changed the subject and wanted to compare what the old Gypsy fortune-teller at Fukushimaya said about my future writing: "I am thinking about writing a book. Should I write a book for adults, or should I write one for children?"

He said, "What you write and will sell well is a book for adults. Even though I say this, you will probably write both. You wrote one about three years ago, didn't you? And until today, you were blessed with the opportunity to publish many books. You are letting those chances slip by. It would have been very good if you had published many books then. However, from now on, you will probably be engaged in this work for a long time."

I gasped! It was because I knew if what had happened in the past was correct or not. I had published a compilation of my writing, *Shadow of The Heart* in 1939. Then in March 1941, when I returned to Japan, I had shown Kume Masao Sensei a collection of several hundred essays depicting America. He had said, "Don't say anything and leave it with me. I will see that all this is published." That one too, I had been greedily thinking at the next opportunity I would design it to suit myself, but in the forty-five days in Tokyo, I could not fit publishing a book into my very busy schedule.

"Then next question, will I be sent to Santa Anita, or Owens Valley, or somewhere else?"

"Santa Anita. And the relocation will take place much sooner than what you are now thinking."

"When can we return to Japan?"

"Next year, and if not then, four years later."

Ah, ah! Stupid, stupid! I can't stand it if it is next year or four years later. Other than about the books, things which will happen from now is in the future; and until that time comes, you won't be able to know until that time comes.

Mrs. A said she also asked a lot of questions, about her husband who had been sent to Montana, about her house, fortune, relocation destination, and she was very impressed. I laughed and said, "That kind of thing may be so and may not be so. It can't be relied upon."

But there were a few things of concern. When we left to come home, I was surprised to see there were close to twenty men and women waiting in line.

In the English-language newspaper, it was reported in a wire from Berlin about the air raid which resulted in the death of one hundred forty primary school children in Tokyo. The commander at headquarters was held responsible for being bombed and later relieved and has been ordered to the front lines. In Yamanashi prefecture, a bomber that made a forced landing was seized and five crew members made prisoners of war.

April 22

A letter came from my husband. It was a reply an earlier letter I had sent saying I wanted to know the living conditions in the confinement center.

> *"Thank you for the letter and all the items you sent. I have received them. Even though you want to know of living conditions here, there is limit to number of lines in letters so impossible to give details. Further, we are cautioned not to make translation difficult. The barrack I am in is about the size of Bandeni school and has xx number of inmates. On my right is Reverend Kukubun, on my left, Old Man Kurihara, front bed is Mr. Kuwata. His neighbor is Reverend Kajitani. Two away from me is Judo Instructor Iida. His neighbor is Missionary Masunaga. We four Buddhists, Christian reverends are all in both conduct and belief making effort to be models for others. Here we received typhoid shots three times. There were those in bed with fever, but only a few have informed their families in*

order not to alarm them. The average age of those in my barrack is fifty-six plus. Those over sixty are excused from most work, and those who are younger rotate to clean the inside and outside of the barrack, cook, wash dishes, work at the hospital, etc. In addition, a few are on special details (group leader, secretary, mail, rationing, distribution, office messenger, etc.) and in our spare time do our own laundry. And to forget worrying about our families, sometimes we engage in baseball, sumo, stage shows, "go" and "shogi" games, and play cards, but no one gambles. We voluntarily subjected ourselves to a rather strict life, and if anyone gambled, we have a rule that we would report it to the authorities and have that person transferred to the Santa Fe jail. (deleted) hearings starting, but I am prepared to remain confined until the war ends, and the reason is, if I am allowed to go out, then since you were teaching, you will then be confined. If that happens, you being sensitive and in poor health, what will happen to you? Besides, I cannot raise two young girls. When I think only a mother can educate girls, I have to sacrifice myself (rest deleted)."

I consulted with Mr. I. "My husband, for my sake, is planning on staying in confinement, but what should I do?"

He said, "You were investigated that much, and Prosecutor Palmer authorized you to stay, so once you go inland, it is a problem that will naturally go away. Write to your husband and tell him to make an effort to get out."

So I hurriedly sent a letter by registered air mail, telling him, "You should not make an effort to stay confined for my sake. I have been investigated and set free and probably will not be confined because you have been released—in any event, let us let things occur as they will and should testify openly, and I do not want you to make any effort to remain confined."

On the way to and from the post office, I thought about my husband's emotional state and feeling sorry for him; tears overflowed. As I was walking, so much tears flowed. I was using my handkerchief to wipe my eyes, and non-Japanese walking by were looking at me strangely. When I came across Japanese, I was ashamed. The other party may have known my emotional state, but fortunately, I did not meet anyone I knew.

April 24

My younger sister phoned and said they had registered moving, so going to Santa Anita will probably take place next Tuesday. Even cutting back baggage to necessities, she says there are fifteen or sixteen. They say baggage should be what you can carry, so large heavy items are out. I asked my sister to tell me the situation in detail as soon as possible if she goes to Santa Anita. Are we going to be confined in a horse track? Until today, we had gone there as a family on a number of occasions to entertain visitors from Japan. If we are put in there, when I think we are not being treated as human beings but as horses, the vexing frustration is overwhelming.

There may be many among the white people who say, "So what? Even horses, there are Arabian horses worth a hundred and fifty thousand dollars which is a lot more than you worthless Japanese . . ." But we are human beings. Humans are the lords of all primates. Just because we became enemy nationals, we didn't drop in rank to an animal. We have the pride of possessing mystical blood and spiritual depth of the East. Who would have thought that war, war between Japan and America, a war that was planned in a world we had no knowledge of even in our dreams, would get us involved this deeply and cause us to suffer? Crime? Where should we look in ourselves to find our offense for which we must be treated like this?

First, we have the same Japanese blood as those who planned this war. Second, some decades ago, we received the same education as they did. Third, what can be determined from my religious viewpoint is that I was born to be placed in this time in this situation because of sins in a prior life—there is no other interpretation that will satisfy my mind.

Evening, I heard Santa Anita stinks with the odor of dead horses, and Owens Valley is a place troubled by terrible whirlwinds of dust clouds.

April 25

It is troubling because I can only sleep lightly. I awoke at two in the morning and could not fall asleep for a long spell, so I got out the sewing translation I did last night and corrected two parts which didn't satisfy me. I went to sleep after that but was completely awake at fifty minutes after four. While useful for burglary prevention, at this rate, I will just get weaker. Others tell me to take sleeping pills, but for a while, I am avoiding medicine. However, I must live to protect my two children. When it is time to die, let us three, mother and children, die without separating. Until then, to neglect our health or overdo things and leaving this life early is against the teachings of Buddha, and we must not do that.

Sachiko again today was writing a letter to her father. In the open space in the letter, she drew a girl's face in a square and wrote an explanation. "Father, please come home soon. I am hoping you come home, and every day I am looking out the window like this."

April 27

The wisteria bloom is almost all gone, and shining young leaves are robustly spreading. Plums are large enough for pickling. The enchanting late spring atmosphere is one that does not leave one without a feeling of excitement, but because of the war, in our society which has now become the enemy, it has a feeling even more lonely than that of late autumn. Nowadays, everyone looks as if they are faces of resignation, uncertainty, fear, anger, and humiliation wearing coats and dresses. In this area, it is not known when orders will come or where we will be sent, so everyone is restless; and while we are able to tidy up and arrange things a little, we are unable to do anything important. I hate this kind of feeling the most.

When I had too much work and felt like running off or when I cried with despair for having so much to do, that was hard; and although the pain was pain, it was a pain that had gorgeousness and luxury. Today's pain is a hateful one containing the dark shadow of pain, sadness, loneliness, and cold.

Being physically frail and living only on the strength of my mental attitude, in the worst case, I could succumb to this suffering and fall ill. But I must not lose. I have children.

Today something to cause a sudden complete turn-around occurred. That was—of Mr. G's elderly parents living in Pasadena—his mother's neuralgia had gotten worse, and they wanted him to come home since they wanted to relocate together with Mr. and Mrs. I. Since Mr. O and Mr. Y's family had all left for Owens Valley, Mr. G was the only male in our house. Even if we get orders to relocate, just I and the children cannot manage to leave from this large house. Mrs. A received authorization to return to her son's house in Santa Ana. It can't be helped, so I still have to rid myself of all this baggage and move to a room in a hotel in Japan town and go to the relocation site from there.

When I asked, there was a vacant room at the hotel. The tarot fortune-teller had said my move would come sooner than expected, and I feel like giving a wry smile.

April 28

The President of the United States announced the following seven main points of his special wartime administrative policy: (1.) The imposition of tax to limit wartime production profits to a reasonable rate (by reasonable limit is meant at a low level). (2.) Control of market price, in other words, this means controlled restrictions of purchasing prices on consumers, retailers, wholesalers, and manufacturers. This includes restrictions on areas with wartime production and rent control in all areas. (3.) Stabilization of wages of all kind. (4.) Stabilization of market prices of agricultural products. (5.) The encouragement of cessation of citizens making unnecessary purchases and encouraging the purchase of war bonds necessary for victory. (6.) Making appropriate rationing system for scarce necessities and prevention of monopolization by the wealthy. (7.) Prevention of installment purchases and trading on trust, settlement of loans and mortgages, and other loans, and if there is money to spare, to have it invested in war bonds.

I prepared luggage I was taking to the relocation site. Since we were limited on the amount of luggage we were permitted to take, I had to rid myself of personal greed.

April 29

Maybe because today is the day we move to the hotel, the children were also up early while it was still dark and folded blankets and packed the dishes we had been using until yesterday into boxes. If we wait until next month, household goods will be troublesome, so we must somehow accomplish this during this month. Sachiko was playing the piano for a while, saying, "They are taking the piano away today . . ." They were all melodies that brought tears. Until today, I had her take lessons for four years, but when will we be blessed with the opportunity to do that again?

The remaining ten items left after storing our goods at Nishi Honganji were stored at Higashi Honganji. I even stored two sacks of rice and was laughed at by Reverend Izumihara.

I had placed a phone call yesterday, and the American from the furniture company came at around ten with two helpers built like ogres. Two large cargo trucks were loaded with mountains of furniture—when new each item costing hundreds of dollars. Including the piano and automatic gas range, all together sold for $75. When beaten down this far, there is nothing more to say.

My oak desk which I had finally decided to sell and the gas stove which was almost in new condition and electric heater were offered $10 more than previously agreed, so I increased it by $10 and let it go. It was after twelve when everything was hauled away. Every room was empty and felt as if there would be an echo. During this time, the company came to turn off the gas and electricity.

We saw Mr. and Mrs. G off to Pasadena and Mrs. A to Santa Ana, and after four, we said good-bye to this house.

Yoko and Sachiko, as they went down the front steps and until they went out the gate shouted "good-bye, house!" many times and waved. It was a house full of memories from early childhood. There must have been many loving connections that were hard to part with. Watching that on my cheeks were two, three trails of tears. After coming to Los Angeles, after renting this house, as a housewife, as a Japanese-language school teacher, and as a member of society and allowed to perform to my complete satisfaction, I cannot help but look back and say, "Oh, house, thank you."

Now, we will never be able to live here again. And for the rest of my life, there will probably never be a reason for living in such a large house. Tears flow. But I must not be fixated on loving memories of the past; we are at war. If you stay in a house on fire, you will get burned—I convinced myself and said farewell.

The two hotel rooms we settled in are full of baggage lying around with hardly any space to walk, and although two rooms, hardly has the space of one room of our former house.

May 5

Last night, I couldn't sleep until around two. And when I awoke, it was five thirty. My body is shivering and will not stop. I wonder if a nervous breakdown is like this. I cannot afford to become ill, but after moving to the hotel, having to pay more attention to my surroundings makes it even more difficult to sleep, and I am troubled.

They say our relocation destinations will be among Santa Anita, Pomona, Turlock, and Tulare; so if you live on the other side of the street from this hotel, you will be able to go to one of those places. In that case, I decided to borrow the address of Mrs. Murakita who lived across the street and use it to register and discussed this idea with Mrs. Nozaki. Mrs. Murakita was among those whose husband had been taken and wanted us to move in with her and gladly accepted.

Around ten thirty, I went to register at the association. I was included in the group going to Santa Anita. Mrs. Nozaki had citizenship and had some convenience and asked the person in charge. Our family's number was 3137. They will be departing on Friday and Saturday, so we asked to be in the Saturday group, but it was overfull since yesterday, so we were denied. Mrs. Murakita had registered yesterday and was in the Saturday group. This kind of evacuation seemed like a spur of the moment thing, and I felt I was being jerked around like a puppet. After five, six days, there probably won't be a single Japanese remaining in Los Angeles.

In today's newspaper, it was reported that until today 996 interrogations had been concluded and released were seventy persons; 292 were released with continuing supervision. The remainder would be confined until the end of the war. We, who until war broke out, had thought we would live in America for the rest of our lives, became labeled as the enemy—something we had never even dreamed of and because of that suffered so much. To this hardship, we lost. And I thought of my homeland where my sons are.

When I quietly think about it, because of the ease of living, to have spent over twenty years living without a care in America may have been wrong. But to be honest, no matter how we consider it, present-day America for the past twenty to twenty-five years has had a higher living standard in all aspects than motherland Japan. And in recognizing women as equal human beings, Japan does not begin to compare. If it were not for this war, my love for this country would have had no bounds. Even if I were to be returned to Japan, after that, what hardship awaits me? If I were ten years younger, no matter how much hardship faced me, I would have had the spirit to just jump over them and continue on.

However, presently being over forty, I know too much of the dark side of human nature, and I would be careful, and I would hesitate. But if I return to Japan, no matter what kind of hardship I face, until today I have seen what others have not. I have seen America and Mexico and experienced many things others have not, and even as a woman have lived without regret, I have had many pleasant experiences and dined on the many dishes of America, Mexico, France, Italy, and China. If I consider this suffering as payment for all that, I can resign myself.

Oh, today is Boy's Day. I wonder how the boys in Tokyo are doing.

II. LIFE IN TEMPORARY ASSEMBLY CENTER

May 8

It is now eight thirty in the evening. I was lying on the bed but felt so miserable and frustrated my head is completely in turmoil.

Just because I am an enemy national and to say this is just a temporary residence, is it justified to put us in such filthy, such stinking, such unsanitary horse stalls?

This morning at five thirty, children in the next room got up and knocked on the door. I had awoken earlier and packed my pajama and things left unpacked from yesterday into a bag and was cleaning the room. After breakfast, all three of our family hung baggage tags that had the number 3137 on our chests. We have truly become enemy nationals. Seven thirty, we went by hotel car to the bus departure point at Central Avenue in front of *nishihonganji*. There were about ten parents of students and acquaintances who had heard we were entering camp today to see us off. From among them, Mrs. Nakano gave a parting speech. They said that as I was giving my reply, from the side a photographer from the *L.A. Times* suddenly appeared and took a picture and left. I was not aware of it; there was some commotion by those around. The announcement had said seven thirty departure, but we actually left at eight fifty.

The evacuees, each with two, three hand-carry luggage, loaded onto twenty-three large forty-two-passenger busses, and moved out with motorcycle police escorts. With this, until the war is over, I will probably not be able to step on Los Angeles' soil. When it comes to the last moment, it seems all sentiments like nostalgia disappear, and everyone was calm. In normal times, only ambulances and funeral vehicles could proceed without stopping, but the busses we were on proceeded without stopping.

At nine forty, we arrived at the entrance of Santa Anita. Earlier arrivals were in a long welcoming line calling out friends' names or waving. I hadn't notified my younger sister, but she was there with Nobuhiro.

After that, we received our room number and the button we were to wear to the mess hall. Our red button indicated we were to use the large mess hall. A policeman checked our baggage; after a while, a Nisei in charge using the smallest military cargo vehicle took us and our baggage to our assigned quarters—Seventh Avenue, Barrack 57, Quarters No. 7—we were riveted to the spot! In all probability, we had been assigned to the dirtiest stable in Santa Anita.

Furthermore, right in front, there was a street lined with latrines. It is so dirty, so smelly; there is nothing to compare to this. I feel faint, and the smell of horse manure makes me want to throw up. "Ugh, we can't live in a place like this!" the children are wailing. Two rooms, each the size of eight mats (three by six feet mats). It is a room in name only. The floor is uneven concrete piled with horse manure and dust. So-called walls are partitions, on which there are countless numbers of crescent-shaped scars. The border between the front room and the rear room has doors with the top half cut off for horses to stick their necks out. The bottom portions of square post holding up the doors are now round from having been chewed on by horses. And hanging from the high crosspieces are countless numbers of strings of dust particles sticking to spider webs of about three inches long.

Mrs. Nozaki went right away to negotiate with the white man at block administration office about the rooms but was told "unless there are more than nine people, you cannot be assigned to the newly constructed barracks. Tomorrow there will be over fifteen hundred coming, and we can't be bothered with each of you." She was coldly rejected. My younger sister, too, said, "Even under the circumstances, I feel so bad for you with a room like this." And she sympathized, but there is nothing to do.

It is noon. They say we must go there by twelve thirty, so we went. It is about six hundred yards away. The area underneath the spectator seats is the large mess hall, and it is arranged to accommodate many thousands. The line of those waiting their turn is about two hundred fifty yards long. One piece of hamburger with ketchup and half a serving of rice. And Chinese tea.

After that, I went to check on our luggage that had been sent. My things were separated at three places, but young men helped me move them near the inspection station. It took over three hours before inspection of all fourteen, including small bundles, were completed. It was very strict, and I had to explain each item, but after all, I didn't have any dangerous items, so all passed. Upon returning to our quarters, beds, blankets, and mattress to match our body count had been delivered. The bed had weak springs, and it seemed you would have a sore back if you lie on it. I suffer from sciatica, so I cannot lie on concrete, and unless the bed has a fairly strong spring, I get back pain. The room was piled with baggage mixed in with Mrs. Nozaki's, and there is no room to walk. If tomorrow Mrs. Murakita comes, there won't even be room for beds.

This is too terrible, and Yoko and Sachiko both burst out crying. Mrs. Nozaki's two-year-old son, Reiho, had a temper fit and started to act up. It is so crowded and so dirty there is nothing that can be done; unless you are very careful in walking, you could be injured and dirtied up by horse manure.

But nevertheless, we decided to sleep and from our baggage took out blankets and pillows and lined up the beds and prepared our sleeping place. When you sit on the bed, the spring sags and sways with a squeaking sound. Tears flow without stopping. It is so smelly and stuffy it doesn't look like one could sleep. However, I must make an effort to sleep. Unless I do, I will get sick. I cannot fall ill at this time.

In the darkness I held my palms together in prayer and silently intoned Buddhist sutras from memory.

May 9

I made an effort to sleep, but the smell of horse manure that seemed to hurt my nose and the frustration that makes me feel I am about to burst drives my nerves on edge and couldn't sleep a wink all night. Last night, they said lights out at ten, so I turned it off for about two hours but still couldn't sleep, so I turned the light on and tried sitting and standing and sometimes lying on my side. Sometimes I gently rock the sleeping children and tried my best to distract my mind and passed the time. If I stand at the door, the stench from the latrines come wafting over, and this too I cannot stand.

It seems the neighbors to our left, fishermen, also cannot sleep and are talking in a loud voice in the middle of the night, saying they should have brought canned goods; and if they were going to be put into such a terrible place, they should have gone to the temporary evacuation site in Pomona. The area near the ceiling is open, so anything that is said can be heard. The door to the latrine to our front is constantly banging, and the noise of flushing toilets is constant. And the baby in the room in the back probably can't sleep and cries endlessly, and I am completely down with a headache.

It happened about dawn. Because of the night air, the cold air from the cement floor came up, and I could feel it on my hips; and my sciatica, which had been well, suddenly came back. My right side is very painful. Tears flow. I wipe it with the back of my right hand. I press down with the palm of my left hand, but sometimes it enters my mouth. Salty! This section of horse stalls were used until recently, and the partitioning walls have horse manure stuck to it. There are also dark traces that look like blood.

Unable to sleep, I tried counting the large crescent shapes of hoof marks on the side partition. There are 109. The image of a suffering sick horse flailing its legs floats in front of my eyes. Just imagining the horse then just died gives me a creepy feeling. Someone said there was a smell of death in the air, but could it be this kind of smell? So frustrating. So sad and pitiful. And unbearably dreary. I am not a horse. I am an enemy national but definitely not a horse. I have seen the world-famous Sea Biscuit and the beautiful way it runs, but no matter how famous, I do not think I have descended to the level of a horse. After all, I am a human being.

However, looking at this from another angle, it means I am undergoing a valuable experience which cannot be bought with money. Morning came, and I left the bed, but I was dizzy, and my feet were unreliable, and my hands are shaking. For breakfast, I had one slice of bread; and afterward, with Mrs. Nozaki, I went to my younger sister's place. It's a barrack, but being new, it feels good. Brother-in-law Yamamoto, with two of his former employees, went to administrative office to plead my case. Mrs. Nozaki also again went to negotiate and was told nothing can be done today, but maybe Wednesday they would consider something. "Ah, that's four days . . ."

We were all disappointed. In that case, I decided to at least get some sleeping pills and forget about the smell of horse manure and sleep and went to the medical dispensary. But I was told consultations were from one to four in the afternoon, and so there's nothing I can do and returned. Then my two children came hurriedly up and informed me that Mrs. Murakita had arrived. I had thought they were coming in the afternoon, so I had not even gone to welcome her.

Wearing slacks and looking every spirited, she said, "I got a nice place we will be sharing together."

Mrs. Nozaki and I both shouted with joy! Mrs. Nozaki said, "Oh, where? In that case, I am going too to see!" She hurried after Mrs. Murakita and the two children. The house was about a mile from the stable to the southeast, with a tree beside it, and the mess hall and latrine were not too far off. They said it was a good place.

After Mrs. Nozaki took Reiho Chan with her to help Mrs. Murakita with her baggage inspection, I went with my two children, and my younger sister went to clean up the newly assigned place. Even though it is a barrack, it is a house that was built to house people, so it must mean I have been promoted from a horse to a human. In the evening, I asked young men to bring our baggage with their truck. It is one room of about twelve mats (about twelve by eighteen feet). We put in six beds. With luggage of three families, this place too felt suffocating. But the smell of new lumber has replaced that of horse manure, and I am happy.

Brother-in-law Yamamoto came after finishing his work as fire warden. He is already tired but helped with piling our luggage, lining up the beds, so at least we could sleep. We are the families of those who had been confined, and there are only women and children, so it is difficult to do manual work. Really, how many miles I must have walked today? And I worked hard unloading baggage, and I am completely worn out.

I thanked Kannon, my Kannon (goddess of mercy), for helping me—I clasped my hands in thanks. Then I got into bed. Everyone, probably from fatigue and peace of mind, was fast asleep like the dead.

May 10

The first night in camp I didn't sleep a wink, but yesterday, I worked really hard and had a good sleep. When I got up and opened the door, the mountain in the east was covered in a haze, and it felt good.

After breakfast, I spread a mat in front of the room and took out our luggage and divided it into things needed while living in this camp and things we would not be using. Then I took those things we would not be using and piled it high, almost to the ceiling, in a corner of the room and shoved the things we would be using under our beds. The other two ladies did the same.

In this camp, there are a considerable number of white husbands and white wives and mixed children. If unfortunately they end up in stables and have considerable distance to go to latrines and mess halls, and they don't like the food, so they are troubled, and there are many requesting to leave. However, they say the policy is that once you are here, no one will be let out for a while.

May 11

Maybe because the bed is not good, I awoke many times during the night. We are not allowed to turn on the lights, so I can't get up and do any work, so I just tossed and turned and waited for day break. Six in the morning, from a room in the barrack where three or four members from the Nishihonganji Buddhist Young Men's Organization were occupying, the sound of a record playing exercise music could be heard, so I got up right away and went to the latrine to wash my face. The front portion of the latrine had wash basins with arrangements, so twenty or thirty people could use it at the same time. The commodes do not have doors and are fully visible, so it is really a problem. One has to take a curtain to hang, up so it is really troublesome.

Around 9:00 a.m., I sent a telegram to my husband about arriving safely at temporary relocation site at Santa Anita. These last three days were so busy I couldn't go to the post office. The post office too is a considerable distance away.

People from around Hollywood are in this camp, so I often meet former students and parents. Most of these people are in the stables, but the stable we had been in was known to be the worst, so I was told by many that all the parents and students were worried. Those who were in stables were affected by a horse-borne skin disease and broke out with terrible welts on their necks, faces, and feet and hands, and they say there is a line of those going to the hospital. I saw many that looked like ghosts with only eyes showing, their faces covered with white oily medicine. I feel so sorry for them. I shudder to think that if we had stayed in the stable, my children who have sensitive skin would be like that.

Newspapers from yesterday and the day before were posted on the barrack in front, so I read it. According to that, in the sea near the northern part of Australia, United States and Japanese Naval Forces had a major battle; and while they are celebrating a big victory in Japan, Allied Forces are reporting a major victory. By being in America, I am privy to strange information that both sides won.

May 12

This afternoon, an English American named Wickensham who is the head of this block came by with a Nisei secretary. Our room has three families connected with religion with husbands taken away, so as is common with Americans, we were treated very politely compared to other families. He asked that we tell him what was needed at the moment, so we each in turn told him that the laundry and shower was a mile away, that we wanted to eat rice and soy bean paste soup and green tea. He said, "We will put all we can into this camp, and when it reaches twenty thousand, we will build you a laundry and shower nearby. I understand about the rice and soy bean paste soup and green tea."

It seems he had been to Japan and China, and he could speak some Japanese, and he used funny Japanese to tease my children and Reiho Chan and made them laugh.

May 13

I must hurry to make the six thirty breakfast without being late. The mess hall stays open until seven thirty, but if you go late, you get fed leftovers. In front of the mess hall, there are two lines—there are two entrances)—that extend fifty to one hundred yards. There are mess halls at seven locations, and they say each feeds over two thousand. Therefore, it seems cooks and dish washers are the busiest persons here.

May 15

Today an airmail letter arrived from my husband.

"The airmail dated the sixth that I sent must have arrived after you left. Saying anything now is futile, but it was very

good that you withdrew Yoko and Sachiko's items deposited in American Bank. There is no choice but to withdraw the deposit with California Bank after the war. It is of primary importance that we do not lose our valuables . . . . Also, at your location, there may be many women's positions, but do not take any and just train yourself as if a first grader, and no matter what kind of person, do not show anger, and it is important to realize the only person that can be relied upon is yourself. Take care of your health, and I want you to stay healthy for the sake of the children . . . ."

So he wrote. Looking forward to a saintly life that extends to eternity, I intend to go on with the aim of spiritual training of myself. I will proceed one step at a time toward the bright light of great compassion. This experience which cannot be bought with money, bearing this life, I am sure that surely someday there will be happiness. I will proceed with faith in the protection of Buddha.

When I went to evening dinner, three women who said they were former readers of my columns greeted me with "Are you Yamamoto Sensei?" I am under surveillance by the FBI. I am keeping a low profile and do not want to be known by anyone, and it is very troublesome to be called by my pen name and treated with such courtesy.

May 16

The chirping of the morning birds woke me. They come to the trees outside the fence of my quarters. For breakfast, a red apple was served for dessert, so I brought it back and made it an offering at the Buddhist altar in my room. Around ten, I went to the dispensary to check if the small pox shots given the day after our arrival had taken. Even if we know it didn't take, it seems we have to go. There I saw a guard and a woman from somewhere having a big argument. The woman had raised eyebrows and looked hysterical. She is complaining the guard had allowed someone who came later in before her.

The guard was a Nisei of about thirty-two or thirty-three. He wasn't very good at speaking Japanese, and in poor Japanese, he was explaining he didn't mean to do that, but the line wasn't very orderly and that is why it must have happened. The woman was a surprisingly good talker and kept complaining. To speak with flowing words like that in front of hundreds of people lined up, I was very impressed, and at the same time I thought she was an immodest person. When Mrs. Y who was nearby said, "That woman's husband must really be afraid of her," I couldn't help bursting out laughing.

May 21

It seems somewhat cooler than yesterday. I was cleaning the room when the young man in charge of work assignments came driving up in the baggage car, saying, "Mrs. Aoki, orders to work!" It is my turn to go on a work detail. I was thinking, *I wonder what it is*, and went to the administration office.

I was told, "Please clean the latrine."

At present, work for women are office clerk, typist, dining hall waitress and cleaning of showers, laundry room, and latrines. Clerks and typists are Nisei girls and limited to those who studied business courses in school. Working as a dining hall waitress was hard work, and there are many who wanted to change to cleaning the latrine since that took the least amount of time.

If I were in better health and also from the standpoint of religious spiritual training, I would have undoubtedly worked. Monthly pay is

$8. I said, "I have neuralgia, and if I work with water for prolonged periods, my body temperature drops, and pain sets in, so I can't do it. There are many ladies who worked in hotels who are looking for work, so please give it to them."

"Oh, that's quite all right," the person in charge said and erased my name. There were three pages filled with names of those who were to be assigned work.

I returned and said what happened to Mrs. Murakita and was told, "That's too bad. You should have given that job to me."

May 23

Very close to our place, a shower is being built; and from two or three days ago, it is under construction, but there are people who come to steal lumber during the night; so to guard it, a soldier is on watch and has a searchlight pointed at it from the roof. As a result, our window is lighted up, and I awoke many times during the night. Mrs. Murakita, who is healthy and energetic and is feeling poorly from her typhoid shot also awoke many times and is suffering.

The radio says German morale is low. They have been saying this many times since the other day. While it is propaganda, they can't say such things about Japan; and even if they did, no one will probably believe it. They also said Russia had a great victory. But is that possible when it is so hot?

From insufficient sleep, I have a slight headache but got up at five. People I know would say, "A person like you is the very person to write and record our wartime living conditions and situation. By doing that, it will also become something we can look back upon . . ."

At those times, I do not answer and only laugh.

At the mess hall at lunch, Mrs. N who is said to have been released from the San Pedro Immigration Detention Center two or three days ago. She said to me, "At the detention center, everyone was envious you were not picked up."

I replied, "Aoki was arrested, and I have two children under twelve years old." Afterward, Mrs. Nozaki and Mrs. Murakita were both indignant and said, "That's why women are so lacking. They should be happy if even one of their country folks avoid detention."

It is a world of women who are wrapped in flames of envy, a world with too many women who have discarded compassion for others. Furthermore, this war has burdened us with a test of a heavy load, so we tend to lose our mental balance and become controlled by hate and envy and other nondesirable things.

May 24

Five thirty in the morning, people walking in front of my place are talking about it, raining, as they pass by. It is a foggy mist and does not require an umbrella. In the afternoon, I went to see Otera Sensei to borrow his sketch of the next men's coat design. He said, "I haven't drawn it up yet. I'll draw it up today. However, since you came all this distance, yesterday I was sent this document from Washington, and it may be of some use to you, so let's discuss it. This is a notice to all tailors."

He said this while scanning the words in the material which was printed in English. According to the document, henceforth, pure wool material is prohibited; men's coat with split back, pleat tuck, matching belt, jackets with collars are not authorized; trousers with large cuffs and length over thirty-five inches are not permitted, etc. It was a complicated thing. However, military items, uniforms, historical clothing, and theatrical costumes were exempt. And after May 30, anyone in violation will face fines and confinement. I think you will rarely see a Japanese wearing trousers over thirty-five inches, but for a tall American, he will have to walk with his hairy shin showing. Shall I say this is sadly funny?

May 25

The radio said last night's blackout was from San Francisco to San Diego and lasted forty-two minutes, but the reason was not given.

Reiho Chan is coughing so much and making rasping sounds from his throat, so Mrs. Nozaki took him to the clinic and had him checked by Dr. K.

He said, "Here we are fed so much meat. He has become asthmatic." I feel so sorry for him, but that is what we are fed, so it can't be helped. At lunch today, I was given a slice of bread with a lot of green mold on it, and it made me queasy, so I mentioned it to the person sitting across from me. Others who saw this said, "Take it and show it to the Jewish chief cook." But I just smiled bitterly.

May 27

Reiho is much better. Got up at six, went to the latrine, and was very surprised. It is packed with people. Yesterday's noon meal of corned beef hash of rotten meat and evening meal of something strange covered in ketchup had affected many; and from around midnight, there were many making continuous visits to the latrine. Fortunately, those of us who shared our room did not touch either, so we knew nothing about it and slept soundly. My younger sister also said it was strange. Ten people were hospitalized, and they say there are hundreds suffering in their rooms.

All mess halls use the same food, so they all had cases of food poisoning, but they say our mess hall got it the worst. If I had eaten it, since I am very susceptible to food poisoning, I would probably definitely be among those in the hospital. Everyone is angry, saying, "Contractors, in order to make profit, purchase cheap items and bring it and cause things like food poisoning."

May 29

Noon, I saw something that was startling at the mess hall. That was an old man with his skin affected by the horse bacteria; from ear to his neck was covered with scab-covered rash bad enough to make one gasp! There is no limit to the uneasiness it causes. I couldn't eat the delicious-looking fried fish and hurriedly left and escaped to my quarters.

Mrs. Nozaki said, "I saw a woman of about forty who had a circular rash of about two inches all over her face and head, and she looked like a ghost."

Everyone says it is a horse bacteria, but I wonder if it is so. It could be germs that are rampant in the unsanitary horse stables. In any event, looking at scabs that look like mushrooms makes my entire body shiver with dread. When I see things like that, feelings of rage rises up within me. From beneath my feeling of trying to calm myself, it reignites and intensifies.

Evening, an educator came to visit and relayed news to me.

"Americans are fearful Japan might bomb them. They have many soldiers in LA's Japan town, and they say they are building machine gun emplacements at various locations. It's probably because that was where the Japanese had their base and wealth."

Then while we talked of various things, he said, "Women don't have to have education. I think it is better for them to be subservient objects of their husbands."

I couldn't accept that so I said, "That's the same thinking as women's colleges. Even women, if they are in circumstances which allow them to get an education, I feel it is better for them to get as much education as they can. Especially in countries with only women remaining after the war, they will probably educate women and teach them skills so that they can make a living without being able to get married."

When I said that, he said, "People like you don't have to worry about national policy. In Japan, they have specialist who do that."

And I countered with "I don't think it's wrong to think about it. If you were an ordinary person, I wouldn't say anything, but we can't have educators saying such things from the pulpit. If I were even casually told that Buddhism regards women in that way, as a woman, I would be lost."

When I said that, he said, "Bah, tonight I am in bad company." And he went home.

When I thought that among fellow educators there are those who regard women as less than human, I felt miserable. Those who shared our room said, "You don't know that person, so you strongly opposed what he said, but he is always put down by his wife, so he probably said that out of spite. They say his lectures are like college courses and completely incomprehensible, and listeners are always asking that he speaks so they can understand. When that happens, he gets angry and says you people are stupid and can't comprehend my lofty ideology.

"In any event, he is that type of person, so the authorities probably saw that he had no ability to lead others, so they let him be. If you just believe that everyone who could be relied upon was arrested and detained, there is no problem."

So I felt that must be so. If I should meet him again, it would be just a waste of energy, so I will not engage him in conversation.

It is a full moon tonight. Mrs. Yamashita said, "I saw this moon and thought of my husband and wrote a poem and sent it to Yamashita who is in the detention center in New Mexico." I thought it would be nice for me to also write a poem. However, nowadays even poetry has left me. I won't even try to try to write a poem and suffer.

May 30

At nine, taking processing papers for boarding the exchange ship, I went to see Ms. Fujita at the social welfare office. There were six others ahead of me, and when my turn came and I entered the room, I was startled when I saw what a beautiful person Ms. Fujita was. She was around twenty-five or twenty-six, tall, and so very white skinned, and her sparkling round eyes were like bells. It was a natural beauty without makeup, and she had class like, for instance, a white orchid. She was wearing a pure white smock, but it looked so fitting on her. I felt sorry to have such a beautiful person in a dirty camp like this.

She was sitting at a large desk in front and doing desk work. There were three secretaries. The one handling my case seemed to be the head secretary and was a friendly person of about twenty-seven or twenty-eight. My request was, first, if the bank says I cannot withdraw my savings, I want the director of this camp to negotiate with the bank to allow me to withdraw the money since I needed it for travel expenses to return to Japan; and second, to have information typed in on the blank spaces on the form. The secretary accepted my request and typed it up right away. And I was told, "Anyway, please explain your circumstances in detail in English and bring it so it can be turned over to Mr. Emory, the director here."

Today is America's Memorial Day. It seemed they feared a Japanese bombing attack, and the guards are paying special attention. The Pearl Harbor attack was on a Sunday, so in America, they are nervous on Sundays, holidays, and Japan's Flag Day. Army Secretary Stimson, two or three days ago, said an attack by Japan cannot be avoided. Around the camp, there are many machine gun emplacements, and soldiers are always on watch.

June 1

At dinner, we were told that starting tomorrow, mess hall breakfast hours would be from six to seven; and to be sure that from nine to ten in the evening to be in our quarters—this was by order of the military—and it was to take roll call.

In the evening, I was making a travel bag when Mr. Nagamori, an acquaintance, came by. He said, "From tomorrow, I will be the one taking roll in this area. Just let me know who or how many are present, and that will be fine. Please write it in here." And he brought an inspection sheet.

"Is this to prevent escaping?"

"Probably so." It was that sort of thing.

June 2

I heard that one of barracks nearby, "a small unit" had become empty. The family living in that unit moved out to join their relatives outside the camp to a farm in Idaho. The unit was large enough for two to three people. I applied immediately, and my family of three was approved, so we moved in the next day. The unit we shared with the other two families was very crowded, and it was very difficult to move around, and we kept stepping on our luggage, bedding, etc. Also, after a long period of time, it became stressful and nerve wracking to live with friends. I can now relax since we now have a private room.

June 3

After lunch, I took the children and hurried to the bank. The bank opened at one, but there was a line over a hundred yards long. The bank handled administrative matters only one afternoon a week, so there was great congestion. It was sweltering hot and around two.

It was the children's turn. A pleasant banker said, "You are able to withdraw your money, and Mother must be happy," and "If you have any excess, please deposit it with our bank." From both, he took 25¢ fee and handed over a total of $299.84.

If I add this to what I already have, it will probably be enough for train fare. Family fare to go east is borne by the family is what we heard. After we returned, I received notice from Spanish Consul General Amot (sic) in San Francisco that the application for the four of us to return to Japan was received and that we would be notified when the ship was determined. I had heard Mrs. Narumi, whose husband had been sent to Montana, had also applied to return to Japan, so I went to see her. She was not in, but her sister, the noted artist Mrs. Kamiyama, was. It seems they don't know what will happen to Mrs. Narumi's application.

It has been almost a month in this camp, and I am getting used to it. I wrote to my husband:

> *"I hear stories about couples suddenly becoming estranged from living in one room with strangers and of one husband who was sent to Texas leaving a pretty wife worrying about her living*

among strangers and asking his friend to keep an eye on her. This is one aspect of camp life."

Today they say at six in the morning and at noon, Japan bombed Dutch Harbor in Alaska.

June 4

Today I am anxious to hear news even one day earlier about my request to return to Japan. Yesterday I received the letter my husband sent with Mr. Asakazu who returned from the detention camp in New Mexico. In it, he wrote, "They are saying that those who return to Japan will have to abandon ownership of any securities. But it could be rumors, and even if true, that is fine. The children in Japan are the main concern." It seems he is worried about our sickly second son.

In the California Bank deposit box which I had paid a two-year advance rental fee, there are eight securities and one security held by the government. Even if current prices are drastically low, even if we make a forced sale, it should come to quite some amount. But having come to this, it doesn't matter. We will probably return to Japan penniless, carrying the rags we entered camp with.

In the afternoon, another letter came from my husband.

"Letter dated twenty-ninth, two days ago, officials from the International Red Cross and government visited our place and in questions and answers with representatives of this place concerning return to Japan, the following replies were given:

1. *The first ship, by desire of the Japanese government, will probably board diplomats in America and those from Latin America desiring to return to Japan.*

2. *Those Japanese desiring to return from North America can board the second ship.*

3. *There is no rule on qualification. No restrictions on age. However, Japanese Americans who after returning to Japan and engage in promoting anti-American thinking or engaging in such activity will be deprived of citizenship. A statement will be necessary to retain U.S. citizenship.*

4. *Train fare, ship fare, the U.S. government will bear all costs to Africa.*

5. *After Africa, the Japanese government will be responsible, so there is no need to come up with the money."*

There were a few more comments written about other questions and answers, so I wrote a few comments on those in my letter back to him.

Yesterday, Japanese planes that attacked Dutch Harbor numbered nineteen, of which four were bombers. They bombed three times in one day. Because of this, it seems security of Japanese will become even more severe.

Resignation and self-destruction counteracting, the ability to think lost, everyone idly drawing their own dreams and living each day—that is the picture of present camp life.

June 7

At six thirty, from the quarters of the young men from *nishihonganji*, this morning music from a record player could be heard playing a song of returning to one's abandoned house. "So many years, returning to my old hometown, and seeing . . ." So nostalgic. It is an old song we learned in girl's school two and a half decades ago, but it touches the heart and invites tears. In this prosaic camp life where one's mind is ready to go haywire, when one hears not noisy jazz music but a song like that, even a tone deaf person like me gets feelings like my soul is being shaken.

Today a crew from a Hollywood studio came saying they are making a moving picture to send to Japan, but people were very angry because they mainly took scenes of Sunday service and didn't pay any attention to the very dirty horse stables. Today it is six months since war broke out between Japan and United States/England. It feels like three years. I wonder where this forest of hardship ends.

June 8

After breakfast, Yoko and I did laundry. During the morning hours, I wrote letters to both Mrs. Sasajima and Mrs. Matsumura. Afternoon, Secretary Hosaka of the Fukuoka Prefecture Association who returned from New Mexico yesterday brought a letter from my husband. According to that, it was finally decided he would be sent to Texas. He wrote:

"Do not be disappointed. Actually, it is strange I haven't been sent earlier. There are various reasons, but generally, it seems those who have children being educated in Japan won't be able to avoid confinement until the war is over. If I go to Texas, I will be together with Mr. Nakajima and Mr. Yokomizo. Mr. Sasajima will probably be sent together with me. To go to the ultimate place and to experience everything is a precious thing. Only from now, all letters will have to be in English. I do not know when I will be sent, but while I am here, please ask me

any complicated matters. Do not complain at any time. To
the children in Shiba (Shiba, Japan), I have asked a friend
returning on the first ship to let them know we are fine. When
we return to Japan, each person will be allowed to carry $300,
so make arrangements to sell one hundred shares of Consolsteel
(sic. Consolidated Steel?) and one hundred shares of Yosemite
Cement and prepare the money."

In reply, I wrote:

"I was prepared for your going to Texas from before, so I will not
despair. No matter what we do, it cannot be helped, so I will
just go along with what happens. About the money to take with
us, I understand. Etc., etc. . . . ."

The clothing of those in camp is really a sight to see, especially
the sight of a pretty young girl wearing a large straw hat with trousers
rolled up pushing a wagon loaded with laundry arouses one's artistic
inclination, but to sketching such a thing might arouse suspicion of
being a spy.

In the afternoon, on the way to do an errand, I met Mr. K, and
he said, "Just now I went with three friends to see old man XX who is
rumored to be an informer for the Immigration Inspector. Regretfully,
he wasn't in. I thought it would be important to see what kind of rascal
he is. He is single and lives in a stable."

Four or five days ago, I had heard there are about ten people who
had their passports taken because of instigation by this evil old man.
Among them was an acquaintance, Mr. YT of Hollywood.

"The immigration inspector said this passport is not yours. You
must have stolen it from someone, and the inspector took it and refused

to return it. I was shocked and dazed for a while. In any event, they must be trying to use the excuse of not having passports to return as many as they can to Japan."

It is really weird. I know for a fact that Mr. T is a passport holder who entered the country legally.

June 14

After lunch, a young lady named Tetsuko, who the children said was a very good artist, visited. She was a cute, petite girl of about twenty who was said to have majored in art at a college in San Jose. She drew a portrait of Sachiko. It was completed in about two and a half hours. It was really a splendid portrait. If I want to criticize, she looked one or two years older, but anyone looking at it would say it was an exact portrayal. I took that drawing and displayed it on the wall with a tack. Around today, an air mail should arrive from my husband; but since it didn't, he may have been sent to Texas.

In the barrack about three hundred yards to the northeast, there is a very tall freckle-faced white woman living there with a baby. Concerning this woman, Mrs. I said, "Probably because of being in this camp, the couple were always fighting, and after one big fight, the husband escaped by hiring out as a laborer at a sugar beet company in Idaho. Then the woman went to the administration office and requested to be returned to her parent's place but was denied by reason that once entered into this camp, no one is allowed to leave, so she is here with her baby. They say on her arm there are scars as remembrances of their last fight."

Since the war began, it seems many international marriages were destroyed. In this camp, there are only one or two white husbands, but there are many tens of white wives. They must be deeply in love couples until death do us part. Being regarded as a citizen of an enemy country, until this war is over, one does not have the right to go to trial; so the husband, knowing that, probably left to get rid himself of evil, thus we gossiped.

Skipping one barrack to the north, Mr. Yokota returned from New Mexico. When I went out to the front, right at that moment, a military cargo truck with five or six people on board came by, and Mr. H who was among them handed me two letters from my husband. One was addressed to my younger sister and her husband. The one for me said to keep doing my best to get on board the second exchange ship. According to Mr. Yokota, Pres. Fujii Sei of the *Kashu Mainichi* is presently hospitalized with high blood pressure but is representing the inmates and petitioning the government through the Spanish Consul General that:

> *"Please do not send our inmates to Texas where the climate is bad, and let us remain in New Mexico. In Japan, they confine inmates with their families and would not destroy families. However, in America, families have been separated. Since we are all under military control, please let us remain together. This is also necessary to prevent our children who are American citizens from becoming delinquents."*

If this is accepted, inmates may not be sent to Texas. Also, they may be sent to join their families. So he said.

June 15

The other day, Otera Sensei said to me, "From next Monday, twice a week during the morning and afternoon, there will be lessons on sketching. I think it will be good for you to bring out the beauty of clothing lines in your sketches, so why don't you attend?"

So around 9:30 a.m., I went to the barrack where classes were held. Instructors were artist Uyeda who had received an Academy Award and Mr. Kuwahara Mutsu who made Mickey Mouse drawings for a movie company and reportedly paid $125 a week. There are forty to fifty students; lesson is sketching flowers and fruits. I asked Uyeda Sensei, "Please include me as a disciple. And can we sketch outside scenery of the camp?"

He said, "That is a problem. The white police say they don't mind, but the military says no. Even then, I will negotiate with them."

The majority were almost finished with their sketches, so I only ordered drawing paper and charcoal and eraser and did not draw. By this coincidence, I was able to take lessons directly from these great masters who ordinarily I would not even be able to observe holding a drawing pen.

June 17

After breakfast, I went to my younger sister's place. She said today was clean-up day for this area and had her sleeping gear out front.

Mr. Kishi, who was one building away, was sitting absent mindedly on his bed and appeared depressed. He was rumored to have seen a ghost the other day. I asked him, "Everyone is saying you saw a ghost. Is that true?"

"Yes, I saw it," he immediately replied with a sigh. So I decided to ask in detail, "In that case, exactly what did it look like?"

Little by little he explained, "It didn't clearly have a shape like a person. When we saw it, it was five minutes after midnight. Around stable barrack number 44, a white cloud of smoke of about three feet came floating out. When four of us who were on guard ran there, saying something suspicious has emerged, that white thing went sliding to the center of the barrack and after a while disappeared with a puff."

They say Mr. Kishi, who was physically fit and appeared to weigh two hundred pounds, was always energetic and had a bright attitude, but since seeing that suspicious thing has completely changed and is depressed and does not talk much. The white people had also seen something, and we heard one carpenter is ill in bed, so it is not entirely a false story. There were some who say two years ago, a jockey who gambled got into a fight with his companions around this part and was killed, so it must be his spirit which appears.

Around nine fifteen, I took my drawing gear and went to the classroom. It was sketching a combination of a plate, bowl, apple, and lemon with charcoal. Saying, "The shape came out well, but it is better to remove the shining parts of the charcoal in this way," and we were shown how to remove it by using the eraser. There are forty to fifty students, but even to me, those who will be helped number maybe ten.

Mrs. Nozaki said, "Today I received flowers to place on the Buddhist altar, and I will share one with you." So saying, she gave me a gladiola with white blossom. In camp, even one flower is precious.

June 18

A letter came from my husband.

> *"Your place morality lost, evenings bad devils a hundred evil deeds, so we hear. To protect yourself, do not step out after eight thirty in the evening, retire early, rise early. To avoid theft, secure door strongly and the entire family of a culprit is talked about and shamed, etc., etc."*

In reply to this I wrote:

"It is a big lie that morality is lost, and in the evenings, devils perform a hundred evil deeds. However, there are those who say they saw a ghost. However, this is a large number of people, so we probably do have young men and women out late at night. However, after ten at night, if one is walking in places other than latrines, you get caught by night guards and put in jail and get sent to Parker Dam. Since I am busy, I haven't even gone once to see the Saturday evening dance. Around our place, we only have those with families, and bachelors live in barracks far away. I think everyone feels seriously about their families. Even those who were disorderly on the outside have changed their ways, and it seems couples are closer . . . ."

Today I heard the following from Mr. M who returned from confinement in Montana:

"In Montana, there was an incident where a detainee was beaten up during a hearing. Mr. S was hit hard on the lower jaw— those immigration agents have now been transferred to this camp and checking passports. These terrible rascals have come here. The interpreter is an unsightly old man over sixty who is a dog (informer) and from before has made considerable sums exposing illegal immigrants and even now actively engaged in informing. Former University of Southern California lecturer Nakazawa was a nonregular employee of the Japanese consulate and halfway through his confinement was transferred to the East, and the situation in Montana must have reached Ambassador Nomura. Then the Spanish consul general acted, and the criminal conduct

of these immigration agents in Montana came to light. The
agents feared they would be fired, but I was surprised to learn
they were transferred here."

Now I understood, the reason why strange incidents of passports being taken away. And I had heard about that evil little old man passed on by word of mouth.

The net of heaven is wide and loosely woven, but none gets by (from Lao-Tsu: "Tenmo kaikai so nishite morasazu")—deeds of the body, mouth, thoughts, if they are not pure, know this! This person will definitely go to hell. There will definitely come a time when the fruits of one's crimes will be reaped.

This morning, the fingers of my right hand itched badly. When I looked, there were scatterings of ringworm blisters on my forefinger and thumb. I was really surprised. It seems I got it in the shower. This sort of thing is clearly a type of camp disease. I broke each blister carefully and applied medicine and then exposed it to the sun for a while. By evening, it was much better.

Today I heard news that Japanese military bombed Port Victoria.

June 21

At lunch, after eating, we were served ice cream. Since four, five days ago, they say our daily food allowance had gone up to 38¢, and the food has improved somewhat.

They say at the camouflage factory, there are some eight hundred young men and women working. It seems they called a strike, saying, "Our bodies can't continue to keep working a hard labor like this on such lousy food." So there was decision to raise the daily food allowance by 11¢.

Now, on the outside, with vegetables in short supply, prices are very high, and one bunch of carrots is 7¢, one celery 25¢, one lettuce 30¢. I feel like saying, now you realize the contribution of Japanese farmers. The newspaper reported that California Governor Olson is worried about the lack of farm laborers and is planning the large-scale import of Mexicans and sent a telegram to Washington.

June 26

Yesterday afternoon, our neighbor, Mrs. Kawasaki, brought over three stems of sunflower. Yoko put the flowers in a large can she found in mess hall, and she placed it next to the window. In the morning, the flowers were pointing toward sunlight. In front of the stables, there is a small plot of dirt. People made use of the plot of land to raise various vegetables like radishes and spinach and also some flowers. Residents noticed the surroundings and admired it as they passed by. Plants are doing well because of horse manure scattered about.

Day before, Mrs. Fukuda brought some scrapped wooden sticks, and so I made two kites using newspaper. I drew a design of Hachiman (good luck saint) using brush with charcoal coloring. Our kites flew highest among many store-bought professionally made ones. Sachiko was very proud.

I was awakened suddenly; the time was 1:15 a.m. My thoughts were whether Americans in Japan are being treated like us and housed in condition such as ours. We are innocent of any conduct detrimental to American war effort. Now the rumor is that my husband who is detained in a separate facility must send letters in English. I wonder if those Americans interned in Japan must write letters in Japanese.

June 28

I took a nap in the afternoon. Recently, I am like the Chinese minister who napped. Perhaps I have descended to the level of worthless dirt. It is because I have no hope. Husband won't be returning home until the war is over. The second exchange ship may or may not come. Really, how long will we be forced to live like this? We have no rights; our freedom is strictly limited; and if we are only going to be fed, it is the same as a dog or a horse. On top of that, presently, thousands have been thrown into unsanitary horse stalls and forced to live there. I wonder if Japan has confined American noncombatants in horse stalls and forced women to use toilets with no doors and making people work for eight hours a day at monthly wages of $8, $12, $16, and $18. I want to know.

After dinner, I took the two children and went to see the sumo ring built near the stables. "Even in sumo, you have to use your head," I could not help but think. Mr. N who defeated five opponents and received many flowers was built like a normal person, but the way he tossed opponents twice his size around amazed me.

The sight of American soldiers in watch towers forgetting about being on watch enjoying the sumo matches is typical of Americans.

June 29

Before daylight, a cat in heat was crying loudly. It is probably the gray cat that was under the porch of the barrack diagonally across from us. They say a male cat goes ten kilometers for love, so this cat in heat must be looking for a male cat and wandering into this enclosed compound. Thanks to the cat, I awoke at five. For about thirty minutes, I lay in bed thinking about how I might be able to live with even a little hope, but I could not come up with a plan by the time it became light.

Nine thirty went to sketching class. It was sketching a combination of magnolia blossom, tea cylinder, plum, and orange. Today I tried sketching with a pencil; it took longer than with charcoal.

June 30

Lately, German forces are victorious, and according to news reports have had victories in the USSR and Africa; but in any event, I want the final battle to take place and this war to end. If war continues one day, then there will be one day of people dying and being wounded. Not caring whether people die or get wounded—that kind of person no matter what country or what world, there must not be too many people like that.

My husband says his crime has been determined, but I wonder just what kind of bad thing he committed. If it wasn't for the war, even if he did wrong, he wouldn't be breathing the air of a prison. To be sent to a prison in the inland because he answered in a way not shameful for a Japanese—can there be something so strange? Man cannot punish man. It is just a way to maintain order in this temporary world. The true trial can only be given by God using infinite wisdom. If alive, someday the day will come when this is resolved.

They say Germany's success in North Africa is by using dive bombers, but from now, many new weapons will probably be developed by both sides.

It seems Missouri University has stopped admitting foreign students. Narrow entrances are being put up in increasing numbers.

The *Utah Daily Newspa*per that arrived today had the following article;

"At Delta, Utah, a permanent living site will be designated and 10,000 people will be assembled there. A twenty-three year old Japanese American U.S. citizen named Robert A. Chino refused to take a pre-induction draft physical and was sentenced to three years in jail. Six Japanese who were scheduled to be sent to Santa Anita Assembly Center were found guilty of holding a secret meeting and were arrested by the FBI and will be confined until the war is over . . . ."

The last part refers to Mr. Sashibara and Mr. Kuwata, block managers, holding a meeting the other day and discussing in Japanese how to get rid of communists and their proposed request to the military. There is no limit to the speed in which dogs (FBI informers) smell out things.

July 3

At breakfast, Mrs. T, sitting next to me, took out sugar from a paper wrapping and also put a good amount in my coffee, so it was sweet. (During the war, there was a sugar shortage.) Across from me, a person named Mrs. M sat with her daughter of seventeen or eighteen. She kept talking to me, so I would reply. When she introduced herself, I tried to do the same. She said, "I know you very well. I have been reading your columns daily for a long time. I had been hoping I would someday have a chance to talk to you. To think it would be by chance under these circumstances".

Yesterday, Mrs. Yamamoto, who is a Nisei and resides two houses over to the right of my sister's place, said to her, "I love your sister's writings, and I brought many clippings of her writings to this camp with me." And showed her this folder that had many clippings. I have many supporters. Even though I cannot see them, helping hands surround me. It is because I have until today believed and conducted myself of that which is proper. And Buddha is also protecting me. I must have courage. When I think like that, a faint happiness is felt going through me.

However, will my kind of writing be accepted by people in Japan? I had written in the style of the early Taisho era (circa 1910). When I think calmly, I get a miserably lonely feeling, like bitter water is filling my breast. When it came to popularity, I had clearly learned it is indeed a strange thing and does not come in proportion to ability or effort. Something I had casually written is accepted but that which was written with great effort, thought, and research is ignored and tossed aside—I had experienced that many times.

July 9

My parent's village in the province of Uzen, where Utsuki castle is located, in the village of Kaminoyama—on a hill to its southeast from where one can look down on over most of the village—there is a house built there called K. At that house, there is a mud pond. I would drain the water from that mud pond as much as possible, and then using a bucket, I take out as much water as possible and change the water all by myself. When I do that, red-yellow koi (carp) and white koi of about two feet in length would flounder around. I would have to catch them and place them into a large cement container nearby.

It is very hard work. I was seeing that dream when I awoke. It is five forty. They say dreaming of fish is portends bad luck. Very cold night air comes through the cracks in the barrack, and maybe because I have a cold, my head does not clear up. After taking one aspirin, I arranged clothing and did sewing and around ten thirty, took off for the Federal

Reserve Bank. Like me, when it involves taking out frozen stock shares and selling it, it must be especially troublesome, and I had called Los Angeles by long distance phone four times; and again, today it could not be resolved, and I was told to come again tomorrow.

Today's radio said the war would be over during this year, or at the latest by next spring, so those who are married will probably not have to go into the military. I gave a wry smile when I thought of those hearing this hurriedly marrying some woman he didn't even like.

Today I heard the following from a neighbor. Behind the spectator seats, there is a large warehouse, and many things are stored there; and among many wooden planks, one had many bad and insulting things about Japanese written on it. Two Nisei who guarded the warehouse discovered it and went to protest it to Mr. Emory, the camp director, who investigated the lumber company that provided the planks and found the culprit and turned him in to the FBI. The manager of the lumber company asked the two Nisei that if something like that happened again, not to report it to Mr. Emory but to tell him directly and left a lot of lumber.

July 10

Mr. Seki who took over checking on people at curfew time from Mr. Nagamori came around distributing the morning paper, but in it, the following was printed in English:

> "All printed matter in Japanese (except bible, hymn books, English-Japanese dictionary) are to be turned in to the administration office by 11:00 a.m. tomorrow. When moved to long-term inland locations, they will be returned, so having them now is not permitted."

There had been talk of this earlier, but I didn't think that would happen, and to have this happen is beyond being astounded. I am really frustrated. This means newspapers in Japanese are not permitted. The *Utah Daily* I had subscribed to will no longer be allowed. It is really too much. I opened the boxes, briefcases, and carrying bags and took out the books. Address book, annuals, *Utah Daily,* even if I throw those away, there are eleven books that will be involved—eight are dressmaking books I bought in Japan when I visited last year, two are Japanese dictionaries, one is a medical book.

When we are subjected to house search and Japanese books are discovered, the owner will probably be arrested for illegal possession of restricted items. They say they will be returned when we move inland, but twenty thousand people are turning things in, and will my books be returned to me without mistake? The dressmaking books, I had planned on reading them when we are settled inland, so I brought them and the medical book so I would know how to treat illness when we are sick.

July 11

Finally, by eleven this morning, we have to turn in all material written in Japanese. When I went to the wash room in the morning, while washing their faces, everyone is saying, "What a ridiculous thing."

"I wonder if the person who issued that order is Director Emory of this camp."

"I wonder."

"Are they doing the same thing in other camps?"

"We will probably find out later."

"I have fifty-six books with me, and they are very precious to me, and I am so worried they might be lost."

"Under these circumstances, soon they might be arresting people for speaking Japanese."

Really, do white Americans think all they have to do is confiscate written matter, and the Japanese will completely forget how to read Japanese or completely obliterate the contents of what was written? How can you eliminate in one sweep what for many decades had been absorbed into your blood, your flesh, your marrow? I want to shout at them in a loud voice—only if you turn the Japanese into ashes can you do that!

It is me, who was a teacher of Japanese for many years, written for the *Kashu Mainichi* (California daily news) newspaper for seven or eight years. I must have read many times the number of books read by a normal housewife. Because of that, my love and attachment for books is deep, and my frustration is great. All right, in that case, I will not lose. I will dig out what I have in the storehouse of my brain. Japanese language has yet to be forbidden, so I will relate the contents of books I know to as many as possible.

Today, within this camp, areas were designated which from now on were off limits from eight in the evening until six in the morning. They say these areas are dark or are places which are isolated, and every night, suspicious activities take place. I had also heard a tale that among the carpenters who come to work in camp, there was a shady character who convinced a pretty Nisei young lady; and in the evening when it was time to leave, they hid under the bleachers and left camp without being detected by the guards but were caught returning to camp the next morning, and both were thrown in jail. We are in an environment where there are twenty thousand people crammed into this small confined space. At least a third is hot-blooded young men and women. If there are a few who are engaged in unethical conduct, that can't be helped.

Even then, why isn't there some kind of facility teaching self-discipline set up? The majority of religious leaders have been arrested, and those remaining are like that person who visited the other night and ran off when I disagreed with him.

July 16

This evening, I made a paper kite for Nobuhiro. I used sewing pattern design with white paper and wrote "Hachiman" on it. It went up fine, but being dragged by a little boy, it soon broke up.

Yoko said with a serious face, "Mother, you are always flying paper kites, so I am going to write to Father about it. He will probably get angry." And we both had a good laugh. No one understands why I am always flying paper kites. That is all right. My soul, which is riding on the paper kite, is looking down on white people outside these walls. Even though my body is tied up, my soul, which is riding the paper kite, has many thoughts, talks of many things, and is looking everywhere. Who can tie up my soul?

I want freedom. Since becoming an enemy person, I have suffered many restrictions in my daily life. I have put my soul paper kites and am continuing to fight. I look down on the world of mortals and pity them. If I place myself in an imaginary world, I can make myself into more than human. Unless I do something like that, I cannot bear to live like this.

German troops that entered Russia are vastly superior, and America is worried the Russian Army will collapse.

July 19

Woke at six. After breakfast, they say the commodes are plugged up. It seems it got plugged up yesterday afternoon, and they used a motor pump to clear it, but it plugged up again this morning. They dig a large hole in the ground and flush waste into it, which then is absorbed into the surrounding soil, but the amount being flushed into it is greater than that being absorbed; so when the time comes, it overflows.

It is an unsatisfactory arrangement, as everywhere is faced with getting by one emergency after another. I have seen where the surface ground had caved in. But surely they wouldn't have something as dangerous as exposing people to falling into a large pit of human waste. The latrine located about five hundred yards to the southwest overflowed two nights ago and smelled bad, and the sound when overflowing was unbearable—is what someone living in a nearby barrack said. Must be because of getting used to toilets without doors; recently, no one bothers taking curtains to hang in front and calmly sit on commodes. It is not getting used to it; it is the frustration, the anger, and the resignation which made women so brazen. Adults look away when others are doing their thing, but little children of five and six stare at people sitting on the commode, so it is troublesome. Parents should pay attention.

July 22

When I went to the latrine in the morning, I jumped up in surprise! From the hole used to pump out waste, sewage is pouring out, pouring out! On to the road, under the barracks, to any low area, this flowing stinky river of human waste, it is the first time in my life seeing a river like this. It can't be helped, so holding up my skirt with both hands, with eyes wide open, with attention on where I step, leaping from island to island, and as soon as I entered the latrine, it was declared out of use.

It can't be helped, so I went to a latrine about a hundred yards to the north, and there too, it was overflowing into the street. It is about to begin flowing like a river. It seems Mr. Kamei of Daishusha had discovered this and had brought out a shovel and made a dike and was trying hard to stem the flow of human waste. The latrine to the west was also closed, so I had to use one about five hundred yards to the south.

At breakfast, this morning they served butter. Mr. M who sat next to me said, "This is unusual. Butter is usually served with bread, but this is the first time in two months."

Mr. K who was sitting across from us said, "The other day, when the inspector was here, there was no butter on the table. It seems there were complaints. They say they can make one hundred fifty pounds a week here. For some reason, it disappears and doesn't end up being served to us. The Jews here are making money, thanks to us Japanese."

Day before yesterday, the inspector came and checked various things in this facility, and it seems he was making a careful check of dining facilities and food. The amount of money being sucked up by unknown food contractors is huge, but at present, we are in a situation of becoming malnourished.

Around ten, a fire truck came; and with its pump, it started to clean up the road of human waste. Our barrack is not close to the latrine, and normally it is not that convenient to use, but we were able to avoid having human waste flow nearby. Wherever you go now, the conversation is about the latrine problem, and I get tired of it. While it is leaking, the latrine is closed. So what do you do? You can't do that?

And even fights have broken out. Built haphazardly and confining a large number of people and overfilling the underground receptacle and back flowing, so nothing can be done. I would like to show sanitation inspectors this creepy sight of a world of slowly, slowly flowing smelly yellow river of human waste.

Even though people may wish to return to Japan because of various circumstances, they are undecided. There is a wide rumor that if one volunteers to return to Japan, they will be apprehended. Therefore, for anyone to volunteer, they must have a good reason. I don't care if I am sent to Japan with only what I am wearing. I want to get out of this insulting, humiliating, melancholy, uncertain life without purpose. I don't want honor or reputation, foundation or wealth; it is today where I have discarded everything. When I look at today where even the slightest hope has been wrested from me, I even begin to hate being alive. But if I am allowed to set foot in my homeland, with a feeling of humility, I will again start anew from the beginning.

Postscript:

I somewhat felt I heard the sound of sutra gongs and awoke. Was it a dream? It is now 1:40 a.m. For the past few days, every morning from a nearby barrack, the sound of a sutra gong can be very faintly heard. When I rest my ears and listen to that unique special "sabi" sound of sutra gongs, my mind calms down and forgets I am a prisoner in humiliating circumstances. Just what kind of person is hitting those sutra gongs and chanting sutras?

In this kind of camp, to hear such a tone is so unexpected, and my soul feels fulfilled. Since I read the writings of Takayama Myogyu's "Nichiren," I developed a sudden liking for Nichiren. It was because I thought that unmatched degree of filial piety, that unusual ability to unify his mind, those points were exclusive and indicated a stubborn character and then some. He escaped being struck down by an assassin because the assassin's horse reared up, but it can also be because he was able to transmit his unifying mental thoughts to the horse that thus was to avoid the dragon's mouth, but just what was it?

Now, unable to read even one book in Japanese, I can only recall this and that of what I have read. At a time like this, sugary fiction does not provide food for the mind. Those that have contents which provoke thought, religious, and philosophical books, those are the ones that come to mind.

July 24

After breakfast, I received a letter from the New York office of *Time* magazine. It is an answer to a query I had sent. It is 40¢ a copy, but last year's issues are 45¢. In Japan, past issues become cheaper; but in America, with first-rate magazines, as remaining copies become fewer, it becomes more expensive. It is a little bit strange.

After dinner, from 7:00 p.m., I went to sketching class. The lesson is sketching Mr. Yoshida. He is an unusual person, and there isn't a countryman in Los Angeles who doesn't know bugle blower Yoshida, and he has been mentioned many times in Japanese-language papers. They say he was formerly a barber and after becoming impressed with the Salvation Army, became one of their members. He wears one tattered uniform and cap all year round, and regardless of weather, he goes around blowing the bugle or singing hymns or reading the Bible. Blowing the bugle, it is not blowing any particular tune; it is like some child just blowing.

Even reading the Bible, he would skip lines or just repeat one part, so it is unbearable. But Mr. Yoshida doesn't care and even lectures to the latrine or tree for a long time. Someone teased him, saying in a loud voice, "After drawing you, it turns out you are quite handsome." There was loud laughing here and there, and I too ended up laughing and couldn't keep drawing.

July 25

Russia, under present circumstances, will be annihilated; or if they run away and escape, their fertile land will be occupied, so it is one or the other, and it seems that is of prime concern to America. It is reported that Japan has crossed the blockade and is sending food and raw material to Germany. I heard that America desires to annex England. If that happens, Englishmen will naturally be in a lower position than Americans; so no matter how dire the situation becomes, England will never agree to that, but the fact that such things are beginning to be discussed is interesting.

Mrs. S who lives in the barrack across from us who was diagnosed with pneumonia was up today wearing a Japanese dress. Her husband is still in the hospital with neuralgia, so the hospital sent two young women to nurse her and look after the children, do the laundry and ironing, and take care of everything. This kind of arrangement is good.

It seems it is firm now that the cooks in the No. 4 Orange Mess Hall will be sent to an interior confinement center in Arkansas in September. Arkansas is known for producing rice, so will Japanese be used for growing rice?

Dinner was mixed vegetable and pork. On my plate, there was a fly cooked into it which was sickening, and I could not eat it. When food is prepared for many thousands, attention is not paid to details, and even the flavor is rarely good.

July 28

It seems an ethnic German-American who came to see Mr. Y today said, "Lately, things have become scarce on the outside, a thing like shoes, you can no longer get what you want."

The children said they heard Mrs. S who is doing much better tell her many children, "We have no money, so if you wear out the shoe you have on, you will go barefooted." Now that it was mentioned, when I would walk by their place, I would get this vague feeling that there was a dark and dreary atmosphere about it. So there were even people without money to buy the children shoes—I feel so sorry for them.

I thought about what my husband wrote in a previous letter: "Think about those who are worse off than we are." I feel chastised. There may definitely be some in this camp who are having a hard time, but then I think of the trying circumstances of Ishikawa Takuboku. In extremely sad adversity, this young genius fell. "On the white sands of a beach on an island in the Eastern Sea, I am wet with tears as I play with crabs." That verse of his cannot be forgotten.

On a vase of Nambu iron, I received as a gift from someone. This verse was inscribed. I do not know where it went, but in peace time, it was always placed on a shelf where I would look at it. The special insight Takuboku possessed and the indescribable innocence and also abstractness generate a sentimental feeling that seems to leave a scar in my chest and generates a strong appeal that freshly overwhelms me. The distress and suffering that Takuboku went through was different from what we are experiencing and cannot be compared, but in any event, but they are both as big and deep that it makes one consider whether to destroy oneself and in that respect are the same.

However, I must not be discouraged. Even though my mindset is one which has lost almost all hope, I must not throw all away and stop caring. I must not give up. That would go against the will of Buddha. As long as I was given the difficult birth as a human being to use my own hands to extinguish my life would be a major sin and would require me to carry that infinite sin with me down the yellow path. Although it has slightly dimmed, the protective light which is provided by the goddess of mercy now provides some little support for me.

July 29

This morning, I saw a very pleasant dream. On my back, I had two wings about the size of covers for bed blankets. I can fly freely in the sky. Then I flew along the hallway of the primary school I had attended two and half decades ago. Small children are frightened and run away. Then I leaped on to the top of a circular staircase I did not recognize. From there, I flew outside, and there it seemed I was not visible to anyone; and even when I flew between people, no one paid attention.

Then I flew into the kitchen of a fine home of an American. On top of a clean shelf were arranged many jars of sugar, honey, and jam. I don't remember after that, but it was so much fun flying through the air. Two years ago, I wrote a children's story entitled "Invisible Cloak," so parts of that conception and the feeling of becoming a kite I was flying last evening—I tend to blur the boundary between reality and imagination a lot—so the two blended. I haven't written a children's story in a year, but when I return to Japan, I might get the urge to write again.

July 30

Mrs. M came to visit and said, "Last night around twelve, a young man walking on the baseball ground was told to halt three times by an American soldier and did not stop, so he was fired upon. He was not killed, but it seems he was badly wounded. It is so in vain to lose one's life in a place like this."

The baseball ground on the side where the stables are off limits from 8:00 p.m. until 6:00 a.m., so relatives and friends have no grounds for protest and are vexed.

August 1

It is already August. Underneath the floor, crickets are chirping. When can I return to Japan?

This morning, Mrs. N said, "Yesterday I received a letter from my husband. In it, he said that for the past two, three days for three hours apiece, they are made to dig holes."

"What? Digging holes?"

"Because it is hot, they drink a lot of water, so everyone has the runs. Remember, when was it before they were taken? My husband once said as a joke if we are taken. I wonder if they will make us dig holes like in the European theater where German prisoners were made to each dig a hole and then shot? But those confined are not prisoners of war. I doubt if they would do such a thing."

I groaned for a while. Then I said, "Aoki never says anything that might cause us to worry. I wonder what kind of work he is being made to do."

After dinner, I met Mrs. Nomura who said, "When Nomura was transferred to Roseburg, he had to walk three miles along the road carrying his suitcase. Also at that camp, they rarely have fresh vegetables, so they only eat canned food is what he wrote."

August 4

Today was a day when the entire camp had a big disturbance. It seemed they are afraid there will be another disturbance tonight. There are many hundreds of soldiers in camp, there is tight security, and there are armored cars with machines guns going around the roads between barracks. It is really strict. Everyone in camp is seething. It became like this because some white police stole and because a Korean spy was guiding today's barrack search and confiscation of things.

Today was our block's scheduled clean-up day, so at seven after returning from the mess hall, we put out the beds, aired our blankets, and cleaned up until nine. After that, I went to the office near the spectator stands to buy a large roll of sewing design paper.

There I ran into an acquaintance, Mrs. Kato, who was there for the same reason who said, "This morning, I hid all cutlery and foodstuff. Yesterday, the police were discussing about searching every room and confiscating various things. It seems cutlery and foodstuffs are among the things that will be taken."

"*What?*" I said, half believing, and was preparing to hurry back when Sachiko came running up panting for breath.

"Mother, you must hurry back. The police are starting to go around, and the neighbors said I should go get you so you can hide precious things."

"Then it is true after all."

Sachiko asked, "Mother, do you have a knife with you?" When I said, "Yes, a small one to sharpen pencils," Sachiko said, "It is silly to have that taken away. There is a police on watch in our block and checking people, so please loan it to me." So saying, Sachiko folded the knife and placed it in her shoe.

I went with only the paper in my hands, so I was checked, but they didn't check the inside of our shoes and said, "All right. Go." And they allowed us to pass. By the policeman's feet, there was a large assortment of bags of sugar, salad oil, various canned goods, shoyu bottle, and things. It seems those who were trying to take these items to their friends' places which had already been inspected were caught at this checkpoint.

When we got back to our barrack, neighbors were all busy figuring out ways to hide various things. But in a small wide-open barrack room, one can't come up in such a short moment with any way to hide something. Mrs. Y arranged jars of sugar, canned goods, and other foodstuff in a container at the bottom of a large community trash can in front of her barrack and placed waste paper and trash to cover it.

When it comes to this, let what will happen, happen. I will gracefully give up all my foodstuff. To make it convenient for the policeman to take away, I lined up one bag of rice, about two liters of shoyu, three bottles of vinegar, thirty-seven canned goods, one can of Ajinomoto (MSG), and twenty-five pounds of sugar by the door. However, I did my best to hide my sewing and carpenter tools. I buried various bladed items in the soil of the potted sunflower and soil of the seeding box; I put scissors under a drawer and under shelf liners, hammer, screwdrivers, small saws I stuffed into three pillow cases and then wrapped down pillows around it and then placed a Japanese porcelain pillow on top and then used its strap to bind them together. Then I wrapped money, jewelry, and important documents around my body and then wore a two-piece dress, so they would not be obvious.

In the barracks with men folks, they are removing flooring, digging into the ground underneath, and burying foodstuff and bladed items. There were also a number of people wrapping books, records, and other valuables in table cloths and hauling them into the women's latrine. The police are men, so they can't enter the women's latrine; so if you bear with the odor and unsanitary nature of the place, this is an absolute safe place, and I admired the ingenuity of this plan. When it comes to something like this, the Japanese unite and help each other to make sure no one is discovered.

At noon, I went to mess hall, but everyone is worried if their place is searched while they are absent and everything taken, so no one is at ease and can't eat. I am too, so after drinking half of Sachiko's milk, which served only to children, I immediately returned.

One wife was saying, "Two policemen came, and if you are searched by nice ones, they don't take much, but if you get nasty, bad ones, they turn over beds and look under the floor, and they say this is bad, that is bad, and take everything. At my place, they took shoyu and a hammer and baby food."

We resigned ourselves and sitting on folding chairs in front, talked among ourselves waiting for the arrival of policemen.

One o'clock, two o'clock, two thirty, two policemen arrived at the barrack to our left. After they finish inspecting six places, it will finally be our turn. Mrs. Y's place was inspected, and they took an electric stove and some kind of foodstuff. Then the next place, that of a young Nisei couple, they took two or three items. Next was Mr. Kawasaki, my neighbor. Mrs. Kawasaki's younger brother operated a food store, so it looked like he brought a lot of foodstuff to camp, so the policemen parked a cargo truck next to the barrack door and confiscated stuff right and left and loaded it into the truck. The old policeman with the sharp nose seems especially nasty.

Three places are finished; three more, and then they will come to my place—so I thought and waited, and then the two policemen went somewhere. Everyone was wondering, "Where did they go?" when a young man from the administration office going by and said, "A telegram from Lieutenant General DeWitt arrived saying to stop the search" Everyone feels like they have just been fooled by a fox.

After a while, like the wind, stories began to float around. At the stables, everyone was sent outside, and then with only policemen inside, they locked the door from the inside and stole jewelry and money. If no one was home, windows were smashed in, or doors were kicked in and entered, and metal things were removed. And if a suitcase was locked, the entire suitcase was confiscated with no heed to protests. One person had $300 stolen. If money was discovered during a search, the policemen would put it into their own pockets. Of course people had seen that.

At a number of places, while at work making camouflage nets, police had gone into their quarters and made off with valuable things. Hot-blooded Nisei were incensed, and tension built up, and there were indications there might be a strike, so they say the white supervisor got worried and called and ordered a work holiday for the afternoon. Also, they say over four hundred mothers who had been feeding their babies at home and had their stoves which were used to warm baby food and milk confiscated, rushed over to the camp official's office, and were lined up to protest.

As time went by, people who had valuables stolen by the police increased, and just money alone amounted to a considerable sum. Officials couldn't ignore matters and had police chief conduct a shakedown of his police, and three who were suspected of stealing the most were thrown in jail. And by doing that, officials fulfilled their responsibility.

It must have been around three thirty in the afternoon. From the south of the camp, excited shouts could be heard. "Something's happening!" People are running. Like an avalanche, grown-ups are running. Children also run. About one in ten are women who are also running. We didn't want to get involved in a dangerous situation, so we quietly stood in front of our barrack.

After a while, news came back. The crowd of many thousand who were angered by today's search had assaulted one policeman and cornered him in the Number 4 mess hall, and they had thrown rocks and caused him to bleed. Moments after that, shouting erupted again. "Something happened!" And again, people are running. They say it is punishment of the Korean, who was using an alias of Kawashima.

People are saying, "Oh, you mean that guy who was always accompanying the police and standing at the mess hall taking notes?"

"Yes, that's the guy."

So it is that tall person with the high forehead. It seems the policeman was not hurt badly, but the Korean was surrounded by about three thousand people and hit with chairs and hit with small stones, so he was injured badly and half dead. He was taken to the hospital by officials, but it seems officials are scared too, and all offices are shuttered.

Not only the hot-blooded young men, but everyone is excited with raised eyebrows and quivering lips and excited ashen faces. After finishing dinner and as I started back to my barrack, I saw American soldiers come marching in carrying rifles with fixed bayonets. And they had groups of about twenty take position around block administrations office, post office, and here and there. Soldiers walked streets in pairs, and cargo trucks each with four or five soldiers patrolled the streets. The police, fearing for their own safety, are nowhere in sight.

On top of having a cold, today's turmoil has tired my nerves, and I am very tired. My hip feels like it is in a cast and has lost its flexibility and feels heavy. My neuralgia is back.

August 5

They say chief of police is known to hate the Japanese. It seems he was incited by the Korean informer and without consulting with any camp official, with his policemen planned and conducted the search. That was why yesterday, the head of this area, Mr. Wickensham had no prior knowledge of police searches and confiscations and, and in anger, left early and went home.

This morning, around nine, I went to the shower and warmed my hip and returned, but it still hurts. I was quietly sleeping, so the children worried and went again to see Mrs. Yamamoto to get medicine and rubbed it on. Then after about an hour and a half, the pain subsided quite a bit, so I asked her to order this medicine for me from the east coast.

From now on, I decided to eat our foodstuff without thought of conserving any. It would be silly to have something like yesterday happen again and have our foodstuff confiscated, and even if we return to Japan, we can't take it with us. I took the sack of rice I had preciously kept without touching until today, opened it, opened a can of crab, and cooked crab rice, and together with Kyushu pickles, shared it with our neighbors.

Soldiers were riding around in armored cars and every five minutes or so would noisily go by. Today mail from the outside must be undergoing inspection because no one received any. Today people who had their suitcases confiscated yesterday asked for them back, and they say the majority did. They say foodstuff and stoves that were taken would be returned in time, but there is nothing definite. It was a day of feeling like I slept through the day listening to everyone talking about yesterday's disturbance.

August 6

There was a notice out that "those who were visited by the police yesterday are to remain in quarters because the military police will be investigating."

At around two, a military police with a note pad and two soldiers carrying rifles with bayonets fixed came; but when they learned the police did not come to our barrack, they skipped us.

What the military police asked those in barracks searched by the police is going around.

"Did the police break the window to get in?"

"Did the police break down the door?"

"Were you in when the police came?"

"Was any money stolen?"

"What was taken?"

Questions like this. Then they are regarding the police 100 percent as thieves. After writing down what was taken, they left after saying, "The soldiers should be bringing back the items later."

There was talk that during the search, one place had whisky which was a prohibited item. Upon checking, it was something that backfired on the police.

It turned out the head American cook at the white mess hall would buy the whisky in town and bring it and then sell it at many times the original price. This was done in partnership with the police, so it didn't come to light. After the military police got involved, security became strict, and they were discovered while unloading a load of liquor from a cargo truck. They say four people who headed the ring were thrown in jail. The nefarious activities of Americans are coming to light one after another. And this in the middle of a camp of enemy nationals.

However, the Americans feel this is a crime of the individuals involved and does not seem to bother them in the slightest.

August 7

The Korean informer who was rumored to have died, they say, is barely breathing at the county hospital. One military policeman reportedly said if he dies, the problem will become much bigger, and it will place the Japanese involved at a disadvantage.

They say he also mentioned that the rumor that the police stole a total of $3,000 was not true, but it was true that they did steal money. It seems it is also true that from the cars of policemen, good stoves and valuable jewelry were found, and those policemen caught with such evidence were thrown in jail. The military police also admitted the Americans who sold whisky were bad people. From afternoon, the military police left, and the police returned, but they are saying friendly things. I feel contempt and frustration.

Today a notice in English came out saying that in the future, prohibited items would be published with the military police doing the inspection, but the date time would be announced when decided.

Officials are very busy trying not to let those on the outside of camp learn about this incident. When I went outdoor to enjoy the cool of the evening, Mr. O said, "The director of this camp, Emory, is the son of Mrs. Roosevelt's cousin and is said to be well educated, but this incident will be a black mark."

August 8

Because of the incident the other day, Director Emory of the Santa Anita Temporary Relocation Center was relieved, and the manager of mess halls, Brewster, resigned. This was in today's newspaper, but thinking about yesterday's paper not being allowed to be sold in camp, the general opinion is that reporters smelled out the truth and wrote about it.

Women were saying, "If that incident were the fault of the Japanese side, the white people would have said, 'Look at that,' and been proud of themselves. The fact that they don't want us to see it, the paper must have written about policemen stealing and illegal sales of alcoholic beverages."

"Police chief should have been fired. But he probably won't get away with nothing."

Letter today from my husband said:

> "My work is, together with others, we clean the rest room and help in the mess hall. It is not hard work. At present, I am 125 pounds. You may not be able to sell the stocks, but if you can't, the train and ship fares are at no cost, so prepare $500 to return to Japan with. There are many requesting to return to Japan, so we may not be able to board the second exchange ship . . . ."

"Father's work is not digging holes," Sachiko said, and she leapt with joy.

Today they say the shower water is unheated. There is no heavy oil, so they cannot heat the water. It seems since the war over three hundred heavy oil tankers that haul heavy oil from California to the East Coast have been sunk by German submarines, and they have problems.

In the East, oil storage levels are down to half; and at this rate, by next March, they will be out. Therefore, factories will have to burn coal. Burning coal will be taking a step back, and they will have to revive obsolete facilities, and this will be a headache.

Postscript:

It is now five minutes after one in the morning. The rain, which started to fall hard from around after eight, can hardly be heard. It must have rained all night while I was asleep. One of my lifetime wishes, which was to live for a while in rainy Europe, has completely fallen apart with this war. Going to Japan, soaking in a hot spring, and regaining my health, I will probably go to work again.

However, looking at it from an economic standpoint, will Japan have the luxury of employing someone like me who has become completely Americanized? Perhaps I should just go hibernate and read and tailor clothes, intone sutras, and write essays and children' stories to suit myself, and spend my remaining days that way. In Los Angeles, I was teaching at three schools, sending articles to the newspaper every day, living in that large house, and meeting with many visitors while raising two children—so I have a memory of a time in my life when I worked to my heart's content, so I have no regrets.

But if we return to Japan with nothing but the clothes on our back, it will probably be a completely different situation. We did not save any money in Japan; we will probably have to sell our land and house in Japan. We have it rented out to a nice family.

In my husband's letter, he wrote, "All things will happen as they will, so not worry yourself about it." In the middle of the night after everyone is quietly sleeping, I cannot help thinking of the future.

August 12

I thought I had forgotten, but I still have attachments to my desk. It was the big, heavy desk that I was finally forced to sell, saying, "After the war ends and I return to this area, if this desk is not sold by then, I will buy it back." It was the oak desk on which I had written over two thousand essays and about one hundred children's stories.

On top of that desk, there was paper scattered all over it as I wrote, absorbed in writing. I suddenly looked at the clock; it was after ten.

There was a class I had to teach at nine, and I had forgotten the time. What shall I do? I was feeling very embarrassed when I awoke.

I have a feeling there was something like that in my past. When I think, perhaps that desk was sold, and its spirit came to say good-bye, tears overflow.

In late spring the year before last, when I went to see the Gypsy fortune-teller, as soon as she saw me, she said, "You are a person who is always beside a large desk," and I was astonished, but I really loved that desk. Even if I return to Japan, if my efforts are not good, I probably won't be able to buy a desk that meets my fancy.

From nine, I went to sketch class. The lesson is drawing the rear of the white mess hall. There was a large tree, and I can't sketch to my satisfaction. While our group is drawing, it attracts a lot of people who come to see. Among them, Mr. Watanabe from the same prefecture said in a loud voice without taking heed of other people, "You have replaced your pen with something like this." Mr. Imaishi of Hollywood also said, "Sensei, you have started something nice." Others in the class who came from elsewhere and do not know me are curious and staring at me, and it becomes uncomfortable; and although I had not finished, I departed.

When I went to lunch, Mrs. K, whose husband was being sent to Louisiana, said, "I received a letter from my husband. He wrote that there were so many volunteers for the second exchange ship, so it may come to drawing lots."

If my husband in Roseburg also comes to that, I wonder how he would do. Since he has no luck in lotteries, he will probably lose out.

August 18

Yoko received a letter from her friend Janet Kim who is the daughter of a Korean doctor. In it, she wrote, "We will be off from school until

October or November. That is because with all the Japanese gone, there is a scarcity of vegetables. So those over fourteen years of age have to grow enough for their families."

I want to go see and say, "See what happened? You now appreciate Japanese farmers, don't you?" If this is the situation in California, how is the situation in the cities in the East? Eating vegetables now must be like eating money.

My husband was taken on March 13, so already a full five months have passed. After becoming alone, taking care of various matters that came up one after another, I couldn't think about them deeply; but as I got used to camp life, I have time to think about it.

I also now understand the life of a widow. The word *widow* itself seems to have a demeaning aspect to it, but I want society to have a more sincere, sympathetic attitude. That is, understanding how lonely, with nothing to rely on, and sad it is. Although different from being avoided as "that's the wife of a prisoner, the family of an internee," I cannot but see a thread of similarity.

That Japan has a system of seeing that the wives of the many soldiers killed can live alone by providing skills, knowledge, jobs, etc., is a very joyous thing. At the same time, I want the proper system to provide them with the sagacity to overcome the many temptations and the proper beliefs with which to provide constant mental stability.

A young Nisei wife married to an Issei who was investigated and confined said, "Living like this all alone—I can't stand this, and I want to do hard labor or even immoral things so I can forget. When I see young couples going even to the laundry together and working, I get so jealous. I get hateful and glare at them."

She was raised without any modesty, so she talks openly about whatever comes to mind and is unruly, but even in those words, there is something to make one think. We can't get by just putting a lid on what stinks and not touch any injury that hurts. There must be a solution. If I am able to return to Japan, I want to be able to work where I can provide consolation to the many widows.

August 21

At 10:00 a.m., I received notice that immigration would be inspecting, so I was to report immediately to the administration office with my passport and the children's birth certificates. I took those documents and went right away to see the immigration officer. He asked a number of questions, and then gave me a boarding certificate.

On my way back, I stopped by Mr. Fedder's office and asked, "Did my husband receive a boarding certificate?" He said, "At this time, we don't know." He then said, "Now, you are to go to Mr. Sano's office and fill in a questionnaire."

So I went to Mr. Sano's office. Mr. Sano handed me a questionnaire and said, "Please fill this in and come back at around one." It is a rather complicated one asking about family, relatives, education, arriving in the United States. I took it to Mr. Sano's office, and the secretary typed the information, making four copies.

After finishing at around two, and as I thought of returning and went by in front of the waiting area, Yoko came running up and said, "Mother, those returning to Japan are going to be let out now to go shopping to prepare. Let's go." So I made arrangements to go out and told the person in charge, "I don't have any money with me, so I will go back to get it." He said, "It is late. Just for you, we will wait ten minutes." All this was so sudden; I was taken aback. Striving not to cough, I ran home, got $150, changed my blouse, and ran back, barely in time.

The group is five people, three families: Mrs. Y and her daughter, Mrs. Kato, myself, and Yoko. A policeman, using an army car is taking us.

We went to Sears Roebuck and a department store on Broadway. I wrote down what we wanted while in the car, asked Yoko to buy half of the list, and we had to buy this in a short time, so it was very busy. When I had bought about $105 worth, Mrs. Y had spent more than what she expected and asked if I had any money to please lend it to her, so we stopped buying, and I lent her all the rest of my money.

On the way back, from each family we gave $1 to the policeman, telling him, "Please buy yourself cigarettes with this." He was very happy and said, "I will tell the camp guard that I have checked all the items that were purchased, so there will be no need to inspect." This policeman had many items loaded on the car, but not one was stolen, so I felt a $1 tip was cheap.

I was tired, but I sorted our baggage. The room is small, and I can't do anything there, so I laid a straw mat in front and stacked the baggage in the corner of the room as they were packed.

August 23

Since return to Japan had been decided, there was no telling when the order to depart might come, so I decided someone would be home at all times. Until departure, it could be one or two days' notice; so in that time, we have to finish packing; and if time allows, I am thinking of repacking things we would not want. After dinner, looking at the moon of the thirteenth night, those in the same barrack gathered outside and gave us a farewell party.

There was a spread of lemonade, grapes, potato chips, cracker, eel's liver, etc. I attended taking a plate of cookies and a box of candy.

And we all talked about our memories of this Santa Anita Temporary Assembly Center.

To me, our family altogether being able to soon board the second exchange ship seems like a dream.

Mr. Y. O. who lived one barrack over from my younger sister's and had been around the world before said, "Even if you are not allowed to take anything, being able to return to Japan, going around the world is great. When you go ashore in Singapore, which is now under Japan's control, you will probably be speechless. When we went there, white people were in charge, but now in addition to Japanese, it will be only Chinese and Hindus. If you are able to get a good look at New York, it's not necessary to see London. It's a dirty old city. Especially since it has been heavily bombed recently, it is apparently damaged badly. However, it's a shame you won't be able to see Paris . . ."

August 24

Morning fog was so heavy that until around eight, from the roof, condensed moisture fell in drops from the roof.

Ah, life in this barrack is only for four or five more days. Those in the neighborhood are all good people, and we all feel regretful about parting. Everything is fate. If we go back to Japan, we go back, and what happens, happens. If we think about it, there is no limit. I am over forty, and I am not healthy; and after being stripped of everything, it will be hard to start all over again. With four children with a casual mentality of an American, I have to make a living in that harsh, competitive Japanese society. I feel miserable to think I have to work for someone else now. I can only strike—and make it or shatter.

August 25

After breakfast, the children took the notice to go to Wyoming and went to ask Mr. Fedder. He said, "You people are going to Japan, so this is wrong. Until you get orders to go to Japan, just wait quietly." I was busy sorting and packing our things.

America is saying the United States had a great victory in the naval battle off the Solomon Islands, sinking twelve Japanese battleships and shooting down nine bombers—and the Japanese are wryly saying, "If you keep losing, morale will go down, so you have to fabricate some victories."

With victory after victory, the New York stock exchange keeps going down, so people who deal in stocks must know the truth.

The German Army is within twenty-five miles of Stalingrad. It will probably fall soon.

August 30

Today the first group going to Wyoming, which included Mrs. Nozaki and Mrs. Murakita, departed. I got up at four. It is still dark, and there are many who used candles to find their way, went to see them off. When little Reiho said in a lonely voice, "Reiho is going to a cold place," I felt like crying out loud.

August 31

It has turned completely autumn. The air is clear and nice and cool. It goes quietly through the space between empty barracks.

A letter came from my husband. In it, he wrote:

"This ship will be delayed about two weeks. This second ship will probably be the last. Even if we have to go with only what we have on and cannot take anything, we have two sons in Japan, so let's live together. Even if we have only that, isn't that happiness?"

If we go to Japan, Japan's wind will blow.

I found out that the departure of our ship was delayed because America wanted to send a Red Cross ship loaded with comfort articles for POWs from San Francisco to Japan, and Japan is saying to load it on the exchange ship. There was a difference of opinion, and the ship to take us was delayed.

Former ambassador to Japan, Grew, announced a fairly common thing that "a strong enemy to be feared is Japan. I lived for ten years in Japan and know the situation well. All Japanese think nothing about dying for the emperor, so they will do anything. Furthermore, Japan is not as poor a country as America thinks, so we cannot hope to blockade them economically. In order to win this war, we must bear many hardships."

They say German forces are six miles from Stalingrad, and it is a rout.

Tomorrow morning, a group will leave for Wyoming. It is group number two. Everywhere is buzzing with going to interior relocation camps. Our fate depends on negotiations between the United States and Japan, so no matter what we do, we can't affect anything. I will quietly wait.

September 14

I dreamed very beautiful Japanese kimonos could be bought for ¥2.50, so I bought all I could carry. Even after I awoke, the beautiful patterns of the kimono were clearly visible in my mind, so it felt really good. It's probably because I am returning to Japan without even one Japanese kimono—and that is at the bottom of my mind.

At around three thirty in the afternoon, as I was fixing a hole in the children's blouse, a young man riding a small military cargo truck came and said, "Tomorrow, please move to the stable." It's true! It is as rumored. The majority of those in these seven areas were sent to Wyoming and Arkansas, and the remaining are only those going to Arizona, and people like us are going to Japan. They will be moved to empty stables, and this area will be fenced off and used to house soldiers. Even then, it is too much. Can there be such a surprise order? And to such a stable again?

When it comes to moving, our baggage is in order, so it is not much of problem, but my sister's place is a big problem. Those going to Arizona will have at least a month to prepare, so they won't be packed. I sent Sachiko to babysit Nobuhiro who had recently returned from the hospital; and Yoko and I, the two of us, packed things that were out in bags, removed nails used for hanging items, removed the ropes used as clothes lines, and worked busily until evening. When the time comes, there is a lot of things that must be done.

Today, with Sachiko, we met Mr. Wickensham, and I said, "I do not want to go to a stable. At least give me a shack for a human being." Sachiko said, "If Mother goes to a stable, she will get sick."

Mr. Wickensham answered, "In that case, I will find you quarters used by stablemen."

At various locations, they have small shacks used by black stablemen. If we get orders to move tomorrow, we won't have to move into a stable. When I look at the now empty room with baggage arranged, I feel depressed. We just do as we are told. For now, I will just obediently follow orders.

September 19

It is five days since we were moved into a stableman's room. The entire area is stables, so it stinks. It feels like the smell of horse manure permeates our clothes, our baggage, and into our skin; so from time to time, I scatter perfume around, but it only works for a very short while. I feel my pride has been severely hurt, and many times a day, I feel like laughing at myself. Because the place is filthy, we are tormented by flies during daytime and mosquitoes at night.

Toward daylight, I caught many mosquitoes that had sucked so much blood they were staggering. Our mosquito net is packed at the bottom of our baggage, and our antimosquito incense had all been given away, so we can only swat them. There are a number of small red blotches like flowers on my hand.

September 24

It seems they are having a farewell party in the barrack in front, and the sound of singing can be heard. Every day many people are being transferred to the interior, and inside the camp, one only gets lonelier.

The last few days have been awfully hot. They say it is because a Japanese airplane from a submarine dropped incendiary bombs on the mountains in Oregon and started a forest fire. Because hot air flows from there.

They say in a day or two, General DeWitt is coming down to inspect, so officials are very busy. Because of that, until the general arrives the mess halls will be serving good food, so we will be well fed. They say it is because they want to say, "We are serving this kind of good food to the Japanese." I hate that. Contemptible! Laughable! I am irritated. It is also ironic. There is no proper word to express how I feel.

If I am able to meet General Dewitt, I would clearly say, "Please look at the stables closely. Also, please look at the women's latrines which have no doors—unless you make a surprise visit, you won't be able to see the real condition of this camp."

October 2

Around two in the afternoon, there was a crowd in front making a racket, so I went out, and Sachiko came running up and said, "Mother, Grace is in trouble. She was hit with a hemp rope by her father and is injured in the face." So I went to the house diagonally across to see. There are many people from the neighborhood near the front door and talking noisily in a loud voice, "Really, they should throw this bad old man in jail."

"Does he have to be turned into ash before his ill nature mends?"

This girl Grace is a cute girl of twelve, slightly older than Sachiko, but her stepfather is an unreasonable violent person who is always picking on her. They say he is disliked by his neighbors, but this stepfather looks very strong and doesn't look his age of seventy-two. He has strength and is always doing violent things.

People are saying, "He is hopeless." Grace has gone to the next-door neighbor's place and is wailing in a loud voice. Two or three women are cooling the face with wet towels. When I went, they said, "Yamamoto Sensei," and the people around made space for me to see the injury. There is a clear impression of a hemp rope from above her left eye to the cheek, with a reddish purple swelling, and it looks very painful. I saw that and said to Yoko, "Go to the mess hall and tell them there is someone injured and get a large piece of raw meat." The meat soon arrived, and I pressed in on to the injury and stopped it from turning black.

Grace's mother was a woman of about fifty. She came in front of me and almost like making a penitence said after her first husband passed away; farming took a man to do, so she took Grace with her and remarried to this husband, but he lacks understanding, so she has not had one pleasant day. Even if she would like to get divorced, she has a child with this husband, so she can't do that, and she kept talking.

Today's incident, she says, happened because Grace was a little slow getting out the store coupon; and just with that, he got angry. On top of that, this happened in front of her friend who is going inland and came to say good-bye, so it is so frustrating.

I told her, "In any event, when you go to an inland camp, have Grace stay with your married elder sister. You will probably be lonely, but you must bear up to it. If this kind of thing happens over and over again, it will upset the neighborhood and in the end could leave Grace crippled. After that happens, no matter how much you regret or cry about it, it will be too late. Furthermore, if something like that happens, how can you apologize to your former husband?"

Sobbing, she said, "Yes, I will do that. My married sister says when we go inland to divorce my husband. I too have decided that."

"Whether you divorce your husband or don't divorce your husband is a separate problem. You have a child with your present husband, so it would be better until after he is grown. If he is not violent, if only Grace is out of sight, you must resolve the issue of Grace."

A neighbor, Mr. S., is angry and said, "Until today, we had to put up with this. An evil old man like that, the neighbors will not keep quiet. We can't stand severe punishments day after day. Perhaps he won't wake up until he's sent to prison. The other day he came to my place, so I lectured him good, but it was pounding nails into sawdust . . ."

October 11

We received orders saying if our departure to Japan doesn't happen by October 27, when this camp is closed, we are to go to Wyoming. I thought about the hardship of going to an extremely cold place where they say the temperature drops to forty degrees below zero. I am overcome. Because it has been a week since my sister has been in the county hospital because of a miscarriage she had when she received the sudden notice about the move, and I had no information about her condition. I know I would get word if her condition got worse.

My request submitted yesterday to go see her this afternoon had been approved, so at one in the afternoon, with Yamamoto, we are scheduled to go to the county hospital. Until then, I made wooden frames for cardboard boxes in preparation for moving inland.

After lunch, Yamamoto and I went to the assembly area in front of the police office. Departure was scheduled for one thirty, but those going to visit the hospital were already boarded onto a small military bus. Eleven men, five women, plus the driver, and two police guards—total nineteen people.

The sky is overcast, and the wind is cold. Mr. Y, of the house of Kanemitsu, is going to see his wife who had a stomach operation.

"Mrs. Aoki, is this the first time going outside?"

"We went shopping in preparation for going to Japan, so this is the second time."

"Since the war started, someone like you must have gathered enough material to earn enough for a lifetime."

"What do you mean? I would be lucky to make even a thousandth of your fortune."

When I said that, everyone on the bus laughed. The policemen on the bus don't understand Japanese at all, so that is helpful.

We arrived at the hospital just before two. It's the same room as Mr. K's wife, so we went with him. When we opened the door, my sister was up. She said, "I'm all healed," and I was surprised. She looks well. After using cold compresses for two days and receiving a number of shots, bleeding stopped, and she is now taking pills three times a day but is almost well; so on the fourteenth, with Mrs. K, she will be returning to camp. Brother-in-law Yamamoto was very happy and said if she does that, she will be able to go together with the family to Gila in Arizona.

At three, we departed; all the passengers put out 25¢ apiece and gave it to the two policemen. Because of that, they stopped on the way back to let us shop, so I bought towel, hair oil, socks, medicine, candy, fruits,—about $12 or $13 worth—but it was all within a very short time, and there were other things I wanted but couldn't. We got back to camp after four; the candies and fruit were shared with neighbors.

Rather than Wyoming, I want to go with my sister and them, so I asked what should I do? My neighbor, Mr. I, said, "In that case, go see the Issei Assistant Manager Mr. Sanno and discuss it with him." So after dinner, I went to his place. He said, "In any event, please come to my office after nine tomorrow morning."

Around ten, when I got into bed, someone was pounding on the door. I got up to see, and it was Yamamoto.

"Nobuhiro has a fever and just had convulsions."

"What? And who is looking after him now?"

"I asked my neighbor Mrs. O."

Wearing my pajamas, I went with Yamamoto, and we hurried to his place about two hundred yards away. Nobuhiro had a wet towel on his head, and his face was flushed red, and his hands were trembling. Mrs. O and Mrs. S were at his side looking after him. They said Mr. O had hurried to the hospital.

After a while, an ambulance arrived, and brother-in-law Yamamoto wrapped Nobuhiro in a blanket and got on. After about forty minutes, he returned and said it was fever from tonsils and was 102. He was given an enema and received medicine to bring the fever down.

We had him take the medicine to bring the fever down and put him to bed. Nobuhiro looked much better than when he was taken. I was worried sick that when I went to the hospital, the children might have given him something bad to eat and given him dysentery or catarrh of the colon or maybe caught polio from Barrack 57 where there was a case, but it wasn't that, and I was somewhat relieved.

October 13

The reason I wanted to go to Gila was, at present, my younger sister is in the county hospital; and after she comes out, she will need nursing care, and my husband is interned, and I have two children, and my younger sister's child is sickly. And using those reasons, Mr. Sanno submitted my request, and permission was granted right away. The feeling of relief from not having to go to Wyoming allowed me to have a good sleep last night. Trying to packing heavy baggage firmly, I used a large saw and hammer and hurt my fingers three places.

Just as I started to go to lunch, orders arrived to go to Gila on the nineteenth.

Around four in the afternoon, my younger sister arrived after discharge from the hospital. Having been in bed for two weeks, she said she couldn't walk very well but looked healthy. Nobuhiro had recovered and acted like a baby with his mother.

III. LIFE IN AN INLAND INTERNMENT CAMP

October 28

We too are finally at Gila, Camp 2. On the night of the twenty-sixth, we were put on a rattling train while being guarded by American military police in uncomfortable seats with legs tucked in and bent over like shrimps and sent to an inland camp in Arizona. We entered camp at what must have been around five in the afternoon. The hateful smell of train smoke which almost induces one to throw up clings not only on our clothes but also on our skin.

Being greeted by many friends made me happy. After talking about our families, the children's school, drinking water, and other things, we were sent to what was to be our room. Fortunately, the room next to my sister's place was vacated about three days ago, so we three, mother and children, were able to move in there.

Yesterday I went to dinner and was surprised reading the notice posted at the entrance to the mess hall warning us about rattlesnakes and scorpions. Oh, we have come to the middle of a desert with such fearful snakes and deadly bugs—that uneasy feeling rattled my nerves and would not go away. The scorpion, a real straw-colored one over three inches long, was hung there. If you get bitten, bind the side closer to the heart as tight as you can and suck out the poison, cool it off with ice, and rush to the hospital, it says.

Before, I had seen a movie about a scorpion handler and thought it looks like a shrimp, and it actually does. Only it doesn't have any flesh on its body like a tempura shrimp. It has two relatively large pincers in its claws. In Hawaii, I had been bitten by scorpions twice; but there, the scorpions were black and small ones about an inch in size, and they weren't that poisonous, so it reddened and swelled up, but I recovered after suffering for only four or five days.

The room is larger than Santa Anita, so it wasn't stuffy, and there weren't any mosquitoes, so I slept very well.

The air at dawn is clear and cool to the skin. Near our place, not having a single tree makes it bleak; but if you step out into the desert, there are large cactus trunks standing alone in places. And there are many stinky bushes with small green leaves called sage brushes.

The mess hall sounds its gong at six. Unless you get up then and wash up and go, feeding time is relatively short, so you will miss out.

The people who work in the mess hall are all Japanese, so the taste is so much better than Santa Anita and can't be compared. And the place is much cleaner.

After breakfast, I unpacked one luggage apiece and stacked it in one corner. Our luggage is all "junky", and probably for that reason, none was missing. Yamamoto made a shelf for storing our luggage. The shelf is about fifteen inches high, and it is so you can spot a hiding scorpion or poisonous black widow at a glance. It seems everyone does this.

At 11:00 a.m., I bought foodstuff and daily necessities at the store. At this store, you can use real money. From afternoon, I laundered clothing which reeked of train smoke, nailed a board behind our room, and made a clothes line with hemp rope. I showered at seven; the shower here can be adjusted for temperature and is very nice.

Waitress at the mess hall, cleaning the laundry, shower, latrine, etc., all have many applicants, and it doesn't look like anything will come my way. It seems the rule here is that if one does not have children to take care of or are not sick, you worked. If I am ordered to work, I will choose farming.

To become attached to the soil was one of my wishes for a long time. But if you go out in the field, there are probably many dangers like being bitten by a rattlesnake or stung by a scorpion. When it comes to that, it comes. I will just resign myself as being born under an unlucky star and die.

Here at Gila, we get the Los Angeles English-language newspaper. It reports a fierce battle going on at Guadalcanal. It announced the sinking of a battleship on September 15. A reporter for the *Saturday Evening Post* named Edgar Snow, who is at the front lines in China, reported the following, and it is interesting, so I will write it here"

> "*Generally, the leadership principle when planning an operation is that you must assume 'the enemy has about the same level of intelligence as you do.' Unfortunately, we and the British have ridiculed the Japanese and have not applied that principle when dealing with them. This is the reason we have met with heavy misfortunes in Asia and the Pacific . . . The error in overly underestimating the Japanese resulted from focusing entirely on their passive nature and did not look at their active progressive side. In other words, we looked only at the Japan of today and did not see the obvious. We said this is what Japan did yesterday and were concerned only with that and did not think even a little bit about what Japan might do tomorrow. . . Didn't Japan become the world's second largest empire? It is larger than the United States exclusive of its territories. And it has a total*

population of 500,000,000. If Japan conquers India, it will control over half of the world's population . . . ."

November 3

Today in Japan is a holiday celebrating the birth of the Emperor Meiji. The Japanese people must be happy with its victories in many places. On the other hand, we have absolutely nothing to be joyous about. It is an unfathomable unpleasantness like we have been tricked. I wonder if the U.S. government listed the passengers on the exchange ship without the approval of the Japan government. Those of us who were designated as exchange passengers were subjected to a list of restricted items we could not take and lost just about everything. However, I wonder what will happen. For now, I will just wait and see what happens.

In the morning, I was trying to make a desk when Yamamoto came and helped. Next, I think I will build a closet the size of a piano. I have boards used in crating our things from Santa Anita and lumber I collected from leftovers from constructing these barracks.

The briefcase my sister's family lost during the movement had been found dropped at the Casa Grande rail station, and around eleven, a young man who worked at the warehouse delivered the briefcase that contained about ¥30,000. (The dollar-yen exchange rate at the time was $1 to ¥4.). The money was not cash but savings. Besides that, we were thankful passports and other important documents were not lost.

After dinner, Mr. and Mrs. Suzuki dropped by and said there were two or three ladies who wanted to meet me, so I said after four or five days when my closet is finished and the room is cleared up.

If going to Japan is not going to happen, naturally I will have to think about work. My desire to farm is fine with Mr. I, Mr. Y, and my sister and her husband, but there are many acquaintances that are against it. Mr. T, Mr. A, Mr. K, and Mrs. M told me, "If you join the news group or something and write for us, we would be happy."

Mrs. M tells me in all seriousness, "Sensei, if you farm, no matter how clear your skin is, you will develop freckles. There is no need to become a farmer now to make dirty freckles."

Freckles? I see. But if they are freckles from farming, even my husband wouldn't complain. Even the death angel who is waiting to take me as its next bride shouldn't mind. It's fine to throw a dirtied-up face and body to the death angel.

For some reason, the stars of Arizona are as beautiful as blooming flowers. I thought the night sky in Hawaii was pretty, but the stars seen here are just as pretty. Lately it has become very cold at night and during the morning hours. I heard that rattlesnakes now come out only during the day, so I have stopped hiking and wearing boots at dusk. It takes an effort to stomp around with boots.

Wendell Willkie has commented clearly on the war and censorship, "Censorship is an arbitrary exercise of authority and undemocratic which conceals the truth and leaves false information and empties air and creates uneasiness among the populace. We should be watching the lack of cooperation between the army and navy and at the same time be investigating the army and navy's propaganda. The ones who are harmed by this are the American people."

He also said a number of other things and announced many things pointing out the faults of Roosevelt's policies. They can't punish Willkie who competed for the presidency, so he must be like a painful itch.

November 7

Today, from morning, there has been a yellow airplane flying around. To the south of the camp, for around twenty-five miles, it is a desert of sage brush. There, they say, are two airfields that belong to Chiang Kai-shek, and Chinese pilots are being trained there. The yellow airplanes are their training airplanes.

Since I came to this place, I have been visited by a number of former students and their parents. This afternoon, a young man named H came to see me from the other side of our camp, about three miles away. It was because two or three days ago, the mother of this young man came to see me and asked that I admonish him. Young man H was a former student of mine, but since he graduated from high school as an honor student, he had become conceited and filled with self-importance. Honestly, I too acknowledge his high intelligence. When I was teaching, he was a young man who would breeze through Chinese classic which I thought might be difficult for students. His mother had said, "He won't listen to anyone else, but he says he will listen to you."

As soon as he sat down, without smiling, with stern eyes on him, I told him about the famous swordsman, Yagyu Jubei. Then I lectured on how it was important to have a humble attitude and study seriously. You have to pound that arrogant, disrespectful attitude out of your system. Using my words carefully with my entire body, a concentration of nerves I talked; and at the end, I wondered if I had been too strict—so I felt and decided I had said enough.

He said, "I understand very well. I will think about it. In two or three days, I will give my reply to my mother. She will probably let you know."

So saying, he went home. When the young man went home, tension left me, and I felt drained.

My two children protested, "Mother, you are mean. As soon as that student sat down, you said those things and scolded him. Any more and we thought he would start crying and were really worried. His eyes were full of tears."

But if I were not really concerned about him, I would not scold him because I know how difficult it is to scold anyone.

It is the rough remedy to straighten out the core of the person. If his attitude changes, and he becomes inspired to leave this camp and go to some university, his parents would be so happy.

November 12

When dawn broke, the wind had died down. Last night the wind blew hard, and in the sand that blew against the glass window, I heard the sound of weaving branches, of blowing leaves, of falling fruits mixed in, which gave me a dreary feeling. In reality, the desert is bleak, and there is a tremendous feeling lurking in it.

Afternoon, Reporter H and Advisor Mr. S of the Gila News visited and prodded me to write something. I was also asked to be a reporter. I didn't feel like it, so I turned them down, saying, "I have volunteered for farm work, so I decline."

And I recommended Mrs. E from Pasadena in my place. I don't know exactly what she looks like, but I had read her writing a number of times. Her real occupation is a piano teacher. The two were disappointed and left, saying, "In that case, we will come again."

Sachiko said, "You are being asked so much. Mother, you should write for everyone." So I asked why? She said, "Like in the mess hall, many men and women, say your mother, should write for us—they tell us."

I gave a wry smile.

After dinner, Mr. and Mrs. N said, "Please write for us in the Gila News."

Today, for some reason, I am being asked many times. I may be called disrespectful, or I may be called stubborn, but what I don't want to do I don't want to do. If one is popular, there exists envious eyes of others, and eventually you will be exposed to peril. In my present circumstances, I must put safety first. In that respect, farming is the most unassuming and safe zone.

From Mrs. H of our camp, I received words of thanks that young man H who had been lectured by me the other day had decided to enroll at a technical university in Chicago and had resumed studying.

November 14

Mr. T, an agent for the *Weekly Rocky News* asked me to write something. "No!" I snapped back, but Mr. T is very persistent. He jabbered about many things, and I became annoyed and looked away. In my mind, I thought one must be careful talking to a person like this.

The other evening, at the shower, a pregnant young lady greeted me, saying, "You're the one that wrote for the *Kamai* newspaper, aren't you? I liked your fairy tales and enjoyed reading them on Sundays."

At the time, I felt very happy somehow. If it was about my essays, it is one thing, but this person talked to me about children's stories. To think, people like to read my fairy tales—I became warm inside.

Yesterday, Mr. XX said, "I thought women writers would be smoking and loafing around, but I was surprised because it doesn't seem like you smoke, and whenever I see you, you are busy working."

This is so stupid! But thinking like that is old-time notions. If one hope to write something good, one has to do things themselves, and as much experience as possible is necessary. Even if one lines up beautiful words and phrases, if they are not true, readers will not follow. If it is truth that penetrates into the soul, readers will not tire of it. That I know very well. Years of experience teaches these things. When someone like Mr. XX says things like that to one's face, I thought there was something wrong with him, and I just smiled and ignored him and continued working.

When I said I was going to farm, Mrs. X and Mrs. Y also said they would farm. That is fine, but when my younger sister said she was also going to, I strongly opposed. She has a young child, and she is still recovering from her illness.

November 24

It has become cold.

There is nothing like lack of hope to make daily living wearisome. Even when morning comes, there is absolutely no pleasure.

Once, I wrote a children's story about a man who experienced all the pleasures in the world and then wanted to experience dying, but I cannot have adoration or hope for death. There are many tasks I want to do than lying around, but I am a coward and cannot start anything new. Ah, it is useless to sigh, but every day I sigh dozens of times.

Broken heart—that is not a word limited for only when one loses a lover. My feeling at the moment is just that, brokenhearted! My heart is scarred deeply, and there is no way to assuage or mend it. Where I am headed, there is only a large extended grey hand of disappointment. There is a completely dry, unpleasant air constantly enveloping me. Even when I go to the mess hall, lately I don't talk to anyone. I am in deep thought and breaking little pieces of bread and eating, and on occasions, I realize I am the only one left at the table and get up in surprise.

Going in and out of the mess hall and on the street when we pass by, there is a lady that looks at me coldly. She looks very high-strung with pale skin and is around thirty-two or thirty-three. The children say they had noticed from before, but I had only begun to think this was strange from one or two days ago. She is a complete stranger with whom I have no obligations or grudge. It may be because many people talk to me, and the waitresses (all wives from fine families) would often give me special service, but I do not know the real reason.

December 1

I got up in the morning, and when I went out and looked, there were six large magnificent daikon wrapped in newspaper with half their faces showing on the porch. When I thought that even in a camp like this an anonymous giver had appeared, I was happy but also felt sorry. Prior to the war, I received gifts from anonymous givers frequently. Vegetables, fruits, flowers, plants, etc., and sometimes there would be *waka* (five-seven-five-seven-seven-syllable poems) and haiku (five-seven-five-syllable poems) attached. There was a time I wrote that I liked white chrysanthemums and received many at once from many fans and felt I shouldn't have written that.

Even if I want to be a farmer, it is December, and they say there will be no increase of farm workers. It can't be helped, and I will have to wait until next spring when planting season begins.

I started a movement to bring those confined (confined in Department of Justice Detention Centers) and their families back together. I believe this is definitely a worthy cause, so I will engage in it with conviction. I received a copy of a list of families and addresses of families of those confined, and among those listed, I surveyed a number of those I knew, and all were greatly in favor. This is an inland camp, so even if I engage in a group activity, there is no reason I would be arrested.

It so happened that when I visited Mrs. N at her place, she proposed consulting with a lawyer and preparing a request to bring families together. So I visited Mr. M and was told, "That kind of thing is fine, but in my opinion, I have no idea how effective it will be. About a week ago, Washington sent a lawyer named Mr. Talley to this camp. Let's go talk to him."

So I went with Mr. M to the administration office.

Talley was leaning back in his chair with his feet on his desk in a very impolite manner and appeared bored. Just when we went there, they were installing an electric heater, and I felt very envious.

Mr. Talley heard my proposal and said, "If one hundred and one families sign one petition, all would have the same status and will have to wait until facilities are built in the camp to accommodate them all. The government will place them as soon as each facility is completed, so it is better for each one to sign individual petitions. Then if applications are accepted in order of received, then it is better to apply early. Today you came, so I will write a letter to Mr. Addison who is in charge of such matters in Washington."

Then Mr. Talley wrote down where my husband was confined, name, my address, the two children's name, ages and that we had applied to return to Japan.

I said thank you and went out, and Mr. M said, "I think you should tell those you know what was said. And what do you think about having Mr. Talley work on this for us?"

I was appreciative of Mr. M who had gone with me and given me various advice. After we parted, I went to Mrs. Kawamoto's place to inform her because she had said, "If you are going to provide such service, I will at least be your messenger and will walk for you."

Next, I informed Mrs. Muramatsu who had said, "We have to show appreciation to you for all the effort you are making for us."

But I haven't the slightest expectation of receiving any show of appreciation. Even Mrs. Iwomoto, who was not a family of a detainee, said, "If there is anything we can do, please let us assist." And that was really appreciated.

December 7

It is one year since the outbreak of war. I am filled with deep emotion. From morning, everywhere they are talking about what happened a year ago.

By the surprise attack, being designated an enemy national, being thrown many hardships one after another, of course not having any mental respite, we weren't even given any time to rest physically.

Losing our jobs, having no means of earning any money, losing our base, our furniture gone somewhere, the security of our wealth unknown, husband arrested and taken away, being shunned as a family of an internee, with two little girls having to move up to now six times, just thinking about it is a continuing agony. To recover from the deep wound in my heart, how many years after this war is over will it take?

According to the English-language newspaper, "Today is the dishonorable day the war broke out." Secretary Knox will publish losses at Pearl Harbor to the extent it does not aid the enemy. In another article, it said America's secret weapon is the $22.200 billion worth of gold stored deep in mountains of Kentucky. It is now proving very useful on the battlefield. In North Africa, for guiding American airmen crashing in the desert back to their bases, for one airman, $5; if together with parachute, a $10 gold piece is given. It was written that during the civil war in Spain, it was used in various ways and that even enemy generals were bribed with gold.

Reading this article, if it was Japan, even if they did something like this, in all cases, it would not be announced to the public—I thought on this kind of thing America is very open.

Yoko said, "Mother, is it because of this kind of camp that you cannot write? Someday, when you can write gain, please write children's stories for us. And tell us about it."

But in this sad and desolate existence, it would be too difficult to write children's stories that would not spoil their dreams.

December 16

I caught a cold two or three days ago and was suffering terribly. My ears are ringing, but I put up with it and got up. It is sad that I work in this condition, but when I am not working, it is hard for my children to see me as if I had lost my will to survive. Until I had heard them enviously say numerous times how at so-and-so's place, the father, the mother, the son and daughter are all working. The other day, my sister laughingly told me even Nobuhiro had said, "Mother, you should work."

Until the war, brother-in-law Yamamoto had operated five fruit/vegetable stores and had a large income every month; he is not complaining and is just a dishwasher. He is working at the Block 32 mess hall. Doctors and heads of work departments receive $19 a month; all others receive $16. The children who do not know that at present, monthly pay is not the standard for measuring one's ability or skill just think everyone should work.

After taking one aspirin at lunchtime, I walked over a mile and a half in sandstorm to work at the hospital barrack. The work entailed using sewing machine to make surgical gowns, curtains, and large and small bags. I worked with a young lady who was previously my student at sewing class in Los Angeles. The task was exhausting. I utilized approximately two hundred yards of fabric during the day, and by 4:00 p.m., I felt dizzy. Young girls take many rest breaks, and so they seemed alright.

Next day during lunch, a young man approached me and told me I should not be working so hard. He said, "If I were the foreman, I would obtain five more sewing machines and operators to handle the workload." I thanked him. "I see you were educated in Japan." He replied he had attended elementary school and one year of high school but did not learn much. He is now working as a janitor at the hospital. As for myself, I have to keep working to make ends meet. However, I had to quit because there was much dust and pollen in the air. I had difficulty breathing and suffered from a sore throat.

December 21

Because of my poor health, I resigned from the sewing job after having worked two weeks. Sachiko was concerned that I had quit the job and thereby dealing with the loss of income. But I had to take care of my body first. What good is it if I were to pass away right now?

Lately, Roosevelt has been saying the America and England's objectives of this war are for: (1) freedom of speech; (2) freedom of religion; (3) freedom from fear; (4) freedom from want; and these four freedoms are the principles with which the new world will be established.

December 23

After breakfast, I went home, and Mrs. Iohara said, "There is something I want to tell you, so please come to my place." So I went.

She said, "To tell the truth, lately I have been learning haiku from Sakurai Sensei. And I have been given two subjects to compose, bonfire and Christmas. Can you write them for me? The other day, the subject was Hyuga bokko, and I composed, 'Hyuga bokko, surprised at the noon bell,' and Sensei said, 'This is like *senryu* (witty).' This time, I want one composed by you so that I could be praised."

This is really lovingly childish. She is a graduate of the established Fukuoka Women's Teachers' College, so she must know that; she might be teasing me.

"For the one about a bonfire, I wrote about building a bonfire and the wife burying two sweet potatoes in the ashes, and my husband really laughed and said the scene of a beautiful young wife burying two sweet potatoes in the hot ashes, one for herself and for her husband, should be good," she seriously said, which I thought was so funny I could not stop laughing for a while.

I said, "If it were a *waka* maybe I could ghostwrite one, but haiku is, well, please forgive me. Instead, the next time you go for your lesson, I will accompany you. Although Mr. Sakurai knows me so, it will be slightly awkward."

It's true that I cannot write poetry and haiku. At lunch, Mrs. Iohara and her husband were sitting at the table across from mine, and I thought about the haiku conversation we had had earlier, and I felt this strong urge to laugh and couldn't eat. I would take a bite and laugh, take another bite and look off to the side and laugh—and those sitting at our table were all giving me strange looks. I had never laughed like this recently.

The prediction of when this war will end by the Americans is good. It seems the U.S. British side will win. Italy is the weakest, so it will be defeated in July or August of 1943. Germany will lose by the winter of 1943 or at the latest by summer of 1944 and Japan by the end of 1944 or during 1946. By the attack on Pearl Harbor, Japan's strength became known; and by former ambassador to Japan Grew's loud warning of "Know Japan," it seems Americans now understand Japan is not an underling of Germany. And while neither the master of Germany, Japan is capable of conducting war by itself.

December 28

They say the sixty fields of the farm were off from the twenty-fourth until yesterday. When the seven o'clock bell rang, I jumped into the mess hall and then went to the front of mess hall 34 where the cargo truck departs. From today, I am finally a farmer.

Two or three already there had a fire going. Mrs. XX who will be working at the same field said, "Oh my, you are farming? It must be a joke!"

She doesn't believe it. When it comes to that, my clothing stands out when compared to the others—sky-colored slacks, green sweater—on top of that, I am wearing a brown jacket and have a green wrapping cloth on my head. Those who volunteered from the beginning were provided farmer's jacket, underwear, pants, socks, and gloves. Now we have to buy them. If that's the case, I will buy them when I get back.

Around eight, a transport vehicle without a top arrived. Everyone said, "It's the first time for you, so please ride in the assistant driver's seat." So I got on.

In about fifteen minutes, we arrived at a field about two hundred yards to the west outside of camp. There I presented my papers to the attendance clerk, and my name was entered in the farmer roster.

This morning's work was, the men will pull daikon, and the women are to top it. I borrowed a knife from a shed, walked about three hundred yards and entered a daikon field. I sat on the ground and topped the daikon the men had pulled. The leaves are coated with frost. There are over eighty men and fifteen, sixteen women. This field alone is 165 acres, and the daikon field is very large, and the hundred or so people can only be seen here and there.

After working about an hour, we rested for a while. At that time, everyone is talking about the war in loud voices. Then we worked again and returned for lunch. Washing my face and hands, I went to the mess hall and at twelve forty-five again rode the lunch transport.

This time, the work was harvesting spinach; the men would dig it out with a hoe, and the women would gather and pack them into a large vegetable box. You had to bend over to do this, so it was more tiring than topping daikon. At around three thirty, the scheduled one hundred fifty boxes were completed, so we retired early. On our return, the person in charge said we could each take about a dozen daikon for New Year's *namasu daikon* (dish of finely sliced vegetables soaked in vinegar), so I got a dozen daikon of about two feet in length.

Mr. S who lived in a barrack nearby carried it for me. He said, "My wife tells me daikon is a bother, so don't bring any back." I distributed two or three daikon each to my neighbors. Then I went to Sixty-Ninth Street where they sold farming clothes, showed my farming certificate, and bought a wool jacket, overalls, white cotton socks, gloves, and rubber-soled canvas shoes. In any event, to get a set of farmer's clothing cost about $10.50.

Before dinner, I went to the shower to cleanse myself of dirt. The work is fun, and it is much less tiresome than when I was sewing at the hospital. I am working with soil and vegetables, so it doesn't make any difference how blunt I am. The embracing nature of the soil and the sincerity of the vegetables will surely enrich my soul. Yoko cut the daikon I brought home in rings and cooked it with canned salmon for me. It was soft like tofu and very tasteful.

In the evening, from seven thirty, I accompanied Mrs. Iohara to poetry class, about thirty people in attendance, and Sakurai Sensei gave us many good knowledge.

Today my husband wrote:

> *"It is completely unknown when the exchange ship will depart. Passengers on this ship will be limited to those who have been approved by the Japanese government, so it is not known whether we will be able to board. Families living together may become a reality, so families of confinees will probably be moved to confinement sites. They are constructing facilities, and it will probably be around February, March of next year, etc., etc."*

I will write to the Spanish consul in the near future and ask about various matters.

December 31

Farming is really nice. I am glad I made the effort to become a farmer.

"They say, begging and farming, do it for three days, and you cannot quit, but it must be true. And our boss is such a nice person."

The person saying that was a Nisei girl with white complexion of about twenty-two or twenty-three who said she had returned from Japan after completing girl's middle school. During rest periods, most everyone else is talking about the war, but she is always busily knitting.

There are many kinds of birds crying in the field. From time to time, there is a black bird leisurely circling overhead. There would be small rabbits that are still unable to jump quickly, and it would catch them with its claws. The farm extends to the horizon. The manager is a rich farmer's son from Central California and under forty years old. He is a very bold type of person, and the daikon seeds which cost over three hundred and many tens of dollars, he said "got it!" and paid for it himself, so he sees no problem in giving as many they want to the workers.

There was a lady farmer who said, "Since you are a temporary farmer, and I was born a farmer, I will do the hard work. So from time to time, please tell us stories that will benefit us."

She was slim and pretty, and it was unbelievable that she was a born farmer.

Yesterday we picked green spinach leaves for cooking with New Year's *zoni*. Today is New Year's Eve, so we worked only in the morning picking green leaves by the ditch. An airplane flies lower and lower.

There is a male farmer shouting, "Stupid jackass! He must be flying low like that because Japanese are working!"

It is a large North American plane which Americans are proud of. Farmers look like camouflaged men. It was Mr. K, the head of administration, a real efficient person, who said, "Farmers are so easygoing they will become empty-headed, and when the war is over and they are thrown out, they might be utterly useless."

Mr. M, a pharmacist, had said, "Farming is fine, but having your ears frozen riding a truck in the morning cold is where we are worth 53¢ a day."

Perhaps that is why only a third of us are true farmers.

Today a woman of about fifty-four or fifty-five came over, sat properly, placed her hands on the ground, bowed and quietly said, "I just found out you were the writer for the *Kashu Mainichi* and was very surprised. After the war started and you stopped writing, I always thought you had gone somewhere, and just now, I found out you were here in front of my eyes like this. I don't know what to say—I want to thank you deeply for the many years you taught me many things through the newspaper."

I replied, "I am deeply sorry I could not write anything good." I am happy to be among these honest people who worked closely with soil for many years. There are probably many things for me to learn.

I heard there was going to be a year-end party after dinner from eight at the mess hall, so I went. It was a talent show and very enjoyable. Sachiko too tap danced on a high platform.

There was no soba (buckwheat noodle) in camp, so we each had a bowl of New Year's Eve noodle. With this, the year is over. It was truly a year of many trials. I don't know what next year will bring, but all these dizzying changes occurring in my situation will be remembered for life. Wearing farmers' clothes, riding while standing in a topless truck covered in dirt, and working outdoors—my present appearance— would I have even imagined such a thing until December 8 of last year?

I had once been told by a fortune-teller that when I hear the voice of age forty-three, my fortune will open; and truly this year, I have experienced a lot. Although it cannot be seen, my soul had opened. It has made rapid progress. It has grasped the precious reality and taken the first step to eternity.

It is now exactly twelve o'clock. All the mess halls are beginning to sound the bells welcoming in the New Year.

January 1, 1943 (The Eighteenth Year of the Reign of Emperor Showa)

A new year has arrived. What kind of year will this be? We don't have any spring wear, but our family of three took out the new dresses we had made in preparation for going to Japan and wore them. Then I wore nylon stockings and black shoes with heels, things I had not worn in a long time.

We prayed to Buddha in front of our family altar and made our New Year's prayer. We went to the mess hall at nine thirty; we had *zoni*, three small rice cakes, pork, daikon, carrots, shiitake mushroom, greens. They say the delicious dishes were prepared by a former cook at Kawafuku restaurant who was hired for the occasion. It was very good and satisfying.

Last year, at *zoni* time, even though it was an uneasy time, my husband was with us, so it was reassuring. Now I have to take care of everything, so I have responsibility, and there is no limit to the feeling of loneliness. After breakfast, the two children went to Buddhist New Year service. There were two or three New Year visitors, and I also went around to pay my respects to neighbors.

Lunch was at two thirty. They said there would be rice cake pounding at the clearing at Block 54, so I went, but there were thousands there, and there are so little rice cakes. It was ridiculous.

In the evening, to climb the highest mountain to our northwest, with my sister's family, I took my staff and went. I am not sure who it was that said it, but they say if you pile up three stones, your wish will come true; so saying, "Please let me return to Japan soon" at the summit, I piled three stones.

This morning again, they say at the summit there was a large rising sun flag waving. It seems there was also a flag on the small mountain to the northeast, but soldiers hurriedly took them down. People were saying the one who put this one up today was a fairly old man.

From the top of the mountain, you can look down on the camp which looks like a toy. To the east, you can see field 66. Next to it is field 59; across the road is field 69. They look like large green tatami (straw) mats laid down. And at the end of the horizon, we could see the small white buildings of Gila Camp 1.

January 4

Today they say they are going to make my place smaller. My place, and my sister's place, each have three people and are considered too large, so they are going to make both smaller and build another room. This is also because until the war is over, it was definitely learned my husband would not be released from confinement. During my absence, having carpenters freely entering my place doesn't feel good, so I decided to take a break from farm work.

Mr. XX, who is about fifty, in charge of housing, is a bachelor and has an attitude that is difficult to explain but seems to want to be especially mean to me and cause trouble. He seems a little creepy and is a sticky intellectual.

I felt it wasn't necessary to start with my room, but it probably made him feel good to make trouble for me. My nerves rejected his impure feelings one after another. That's all right. In a camp like this, no matter what you say, a woman will be at a disadvantage, so it would be a waste of time to protest.

The work ended around two in the afternoon. The room was reduced to two thirds in size, so it really became small. Afterward, I put my shelves back up and rearranged my baggage. I moved heavy things around by myself, and so my body hurt.

February 13

In the evening, there was a meeting of everyone in Block 32 to discuss the draft. Mr. F chaired the meeting, and he explained the meeting. The problem was Article 27 and Article 28. Will you become a soldier of the United States and go wherever you are sent? Will you turn against the emperor and pledge loyalty to the United States? These are two questions. The American authorities say if you answer *no*, you will lose your American citizenship and become people without a country.

Nisei who wrote *no* are saying, "How has America treated us up to now? We will not trade our lives for registration papers or citizenship." So if answering *no* is of free will, it can't be helped. But it must not be because of threats by others or under pressure. It says those who use threats or pressure will be fined $10,000 or twenty years in prison or both.

February 16

It is fairly warm. The morning work was pressing down the cucumber seeds we had planted yesterday and placing more dirt on it and removing the lettuce plants growing around it. In the afternoon, again planting cucumber, I got so tired, and both legs felt like they are on fire.

It became time to go home, and as we waited for our transport truck, in front of field 59, a lot of transport trucks stopped, and we could faintly see military police were getting passengers off and checking them.

This was not normal! An incident had occurred!

With four or five FBI agents in each police vehicle, they are busily going between the two camps.

After a long while, our transport truck did not come, so we all got on the small cargo truck; and with everyone standing, we returned to camp. There were two soldiers carrying rifles with bayonets attached at the entrance that said, "Halt!" They found we were farm workers returning from the field and let us pass right away.

They even had a machine gun set up, so I thought perhaps we were under martial law, but inside the camp was quiet. I then heard the FBI was checking those who had encouraged people to answer *no* to Articles 27 and 28 and those who were on a black list for undesirable activity.

I heard that by evening, those who had been investigated in both Camp 1 and Camp 2 totaled fourteen Issei and thirteen Nisei, a total of twenty-seven.

There were two women among the Issei; one was Ms. XX who was a witness at the trial of an assistant official at the Turlock Camp for embezzlement of clothing cost, and the other was Mrs. YY, a mother who wanted to have her only son write *no* and accompanied him to the registration office to make him do that.

February 18

Last evening, there was a block meeting, so I attended. There I heard, "Anyone who demands or pressures anyone to write *no* on both Article 27 and 28 on the registration paper will face a fine of not more than $10,000 and a prison sentence of not more than twenty years. Anyone who is pressured against his will to write *no* will face a heavy fine and a prison sentence of not more than ten years. Anyone who, by his own will, writes *no* will be considered a draft dodger and face a prison sentence of not more than ten years, but for those who have applied to return to Japan, your penalty will be loss of citizenship."

America has clearly announced that it lost the tank battle in North Africa. This is the first time I have heard orderly withdrawal used as an adjective for defeat. Secretary of the Army Stimson is saying soon we will announce huge losses in dead and wounded and damages, so do not be surprised.

February 21

Mrs. M brought a dress over for fitting, so I put it together for her. My sister asked for a summer coat just like mine, so I sewed one for her and showed her how.

Today the verses I had asked Sakurai Sensei to correct came back. My verse on "scarf" had an appraisal: "Wrapping a dream is too skillful." Does too much mean unable to attain? That was a very good comment, and I was impressed, and also grateful.

> *Spring Cold*
> > *The light green color*
> > > *of the seed potatoes*
> > *The spring cold*
> > *Cold day in spring*
> > > *my wife's letter is delivered*
> > *Full of censor holes*

(My husband wrote that my letters always get censored, and he gets it full of cutout holes.)

Zoni
> *Without a husband*
>> *today I am eating*
> *This year's zoni*

Sleeping Buddha
> *Pray a hundred times*
>> *beautiful sleeping Buddha*
> *My karma is cold*

Turning Cold
> *Passing out seedlings*
>> *in the celery fields*
> *The hands are freezing*

Night Road
> *Taking my children*
>> *through sandstorm on a night road*
> *Nothing but despair*

Scarf
> *All my dreams*
>> *wrapped in my scarf*
> *Very pretty*

Shadow Grows
> *Remarkably*
>> *on height of weeds too*
> *Shadows grow longer*

March 14

Morning, I sewed a slip. When you farm, you move your body more frequently, and your underwear is always tearing. Things like this, you don't understand until you experience it. Like I had made a big discovery, I had seen slips with frayed cross seams.

Sakurai Sensei had seen my haiku and returned them, but I feel he thinks my verses are too clever. He is always commenting on how crafty it is. I have become a farmer and feel I have absorbed its simplicity, but it will take a while before I have acquired a refined poetic feeling.

> *Farmer*
>> *Became a farmer*
>>> *planting cucumbers*
>> *In the soil I plow*
>>> *I have learned*
>> *This March*

> *Leaf Bud*
>> *The horse gets scolded*
>>> *for eating the leaf buds*
>> *Hillside road*
>> Abundant leaf buds
>>> *on roadside trees*
>> *Bright place*

> *Rapeseed*
>> *The farmers gather*
>>> *Causing rapeseed flowers to scatter*

Soil
> *Fragrance of the soil*
>> *adheres to the hand*
>
> *And gives warmth*

Spring Grass
> *The grass of spring*
>> *Comforting like a blanket*
>
> *Noonday lunch*

Wrinkles
> *The children making*
>> *Paper wrinkles are sad*
>
> *The widow is sad*

Hazy Moon
> *Leaving my hair*
>> *Undone after showering*
>
> *The hazy moon*

March 18

I dreamt that I was kneeling and trying to stand but couldn't. It was so agonizing I let out a groan and awoke. My legs are hurting from tiredness, and my body is heavy. After breakfast, I had promised, so I went to Mr. Miura's office. It was a little after eight, and I waited for about twenty minutes for Mr. Miura to show up.

Mr. Miura introduced me to Mr. Sloan, an official from the Estate Collection Bureau, to ask about the shares of Southern Pacific stocks that were believed to be lost. Mr. Sloan agreed and carefully wrote it down. After he finished, he said, "I have seen you before."

I thought it was funny, so I said, "I have never met you before today."

That is true. This square-faced, stocky big person, no matter how I thought, was not among my friends. He said, "Your book has a picture of you, doesn't it? That's why I know you." Note: author has written a book titled *Kokoro No Kage* (*Shadow of the Heart*).

I was taken aback. It seemed the color of my face changed. "This is terrible. There is an American like this." I felt like something I treasured had been dragged out and made a mess of. I was surprised that Mr. Sloan knew about my writing.

"What did you do with your school stuff?"

"I got rid of it in a forced sale back to the company I bought them from," I replied. Mr. Miura explained I wrote for the *Kamai* newspaper for a long time. He said, "I know." However, I have not done anything bad—I said that to myself, but I felt something hard and cold was being shoved into me. So that I would not suddenly have my courage taken, I must set my feet firmly on the ground and breathe from the bottom of my stomach—thinking that I went to the field in the afternoon. It was terribly gusty, and we couldn't keep our eyes open, so we quit early.

March 29

In the evening, I went with Mrs. Iohara to the Haiku Club meeting. There was a discussion about the verse of Mr. Yamanaka, one of Sakurai Sensei's senior disciples. Sensei said, "You said you did not want your verse published in the newspaper, but it would be strange to leave one member's verse out, and we are submitting recommended verses from the Gila poetry club, so why don't you submit under an alias or something?"

"In that case, do as you please. If you use an alias, plus use a name that will not identify me."

That was the reply, but we know the verse; so no matter what name is used, so if he thought they couldn't tell it was him, it was so funny.

After a lecture on subjective verses, the subject for the evening's verse was "Haze." We were told to compose as many as we could in fifteen minutes. I wrote six verses, and it was on the high side as far as numbers were concerned. We wrote each verse on a separate sheet and submitted our verses without names. They were commented on, but it wasn't clear. There should be precise criticism. It was commented on as having many thoughts lined up, but my verse:

> Into the distance
> > furrows with budding seedlings
> Morning mist

was rated as among the good ones. I had heard that Sensei commented to his disciples that I was a person who writes verses with witticism, but to compose a verse with the true essence of haiku, one having a refined, reserved, happy-go-lucky, detached, quietness that, I thought, would not be attainable until I step into my grave. When I thought that, I felt disgusted in spite of myself.

April 14

In the evening, there was a meeting of Block 32. First was the continuation of the fish shop. This shop was always sold out by the time we returned from the field and could rarely buy anything, so I raised my hand in favor of there being no problem with closing it.

The second was discussion of the study the government was making to remove Japanese from this relocation center. They say if the ten relocation centers are closed, it will result in savings of $500 million.

1. Currently, there is a manpower shortage, so any kind of job is available.
2. If you get out after the war, returning veterans will have priority, so Japanese will not be able to get jobs.
3. For those who leave permanently, they say there will be an allowance of $50 for those who are single, $75 for couples, an $100 for those who have families.

That is why those who have money and Nisei who are fed up with inconveniences are leaving.

From this block, JS, a Nisei with an American wife, got a job as a car mechanic in a small country town in the East and will be leaving tomorrow. He has two daughters and said he will call his family when his house is finalized. The wife says she has become Japanese and has dyed her reddish brown hair black. She is fairly quiet, and her face is better than average. She lives with her mother-in-law, and they get along very well.

America is saying they will mobilize ten million this year, and next year thirteen million, so they will be using enemy nationals (German, Italian, Japanese) too. This will lead to a strange problem. Those who signed *no* to Articles 27 and 28 are saying, "We can only wait to see how Japan responds."

April 18

It is the one year anniversary of the Tokyo air raid. The U.S. government said it will divulge the true situation and has widely announced that Japan had executed the captured airmen, so Americans are very angry. They are saying, for the next few days, it is better not to leave camp, since it is unknown what kind of misfortune you may encounter. People are saying as a result of the anger, the sale of war bonds may double.

A letter came from my husband. He has completely given up preaching and is transcribing sutras and wants to give them to anyone who wants it.

May 2

During lunch, the block manager, Mr. K, said, "Mr. W, a sixty-three-year-old man in Block 63, went out yesterday morning and hasn't come home. We are directed by the administration to send out a search party, so those who want to, please gather at the camouflage building by one thirty this afternoon."

Mr. Y who was sitting on our side said, "Friday evening, it happened when we were playing baseball. A tall old man said he wanted to go to Los Angeles and asked us which direction he should go. So I told him there are no Japanese in Los Angeles. I asked why he wanted to go there, and he said he wanted to return money he owed. I asked him if he borrowed money from a white man, and he said it was a Japanese. I told him if he walked, it will take about three months, and he said he didn't mind if it took three months, so we figured he was not right in the head, and we talked about it. Then I saw the photo that was circulated, and it was that man. Our sleeves brushing against each other is due to connections in another life. I will also go looking for him."

From Block 32, about ten robust-looking young men went. Since they were going into a vast desert in one-hundred-thirty-degree heat, they each carried large canteens. The search party of around five hundred people was split into search parties, and if they discovered the man or his body, they were to send up a signal. But no signals went up by evening, and the search parties returned.

Mr. W's only son left camp to work on a sugar beet farm, and it seems he was living with a relative. In this heat, those who go deranged can be expected. Manufactures of fans are restricted, and it doesn't look like any will be available.

May 7

Everyone in camp took a day off from work to search, even using an airplane, and searched for old man W; but lost in the sky or gone into the earth, there was no trace of him. We discussed whether he passed out or was eaten up by coyotes.

In the afternoon, a tooth fell out from my lower partial; and just to attach one tooth, it cost $2.50. I work all day at hard labor and receive 53¢ and just to reattach one false tooth costing $2.50 is too high for treatment in a camp.

May 21

Carrots are still small, and to fill one hundred bags, everyone had to work hard.

Tonight Block 32 was putting on a talent show, and we had been told from way before that we were doing this to entertain people from other blocks. So everyone had to participate and having no choice joined the group that was doing the costume parade. I used a sheet from a double bed and made a cloak and was going to be a three-eyed goblin. The mask, I had the children help and had made it two or three days ago. I hung thick white strands on the rain clogs about a foot high which I had it made by the carpenter at the field by giving him cigarettes.

Dinner at five, a stage had been built between the laundry room and ironing room, and the show was put on there. It was full house, and food for one thousand two hundred persons ran three hundred short. For this show, we had donated an average of $2 per household. Everything other than the food situation went well.

The performance ended at twelve thirty. Everyone was tired out and slept well. Our block has a performer named Mr. Shikata, and he was the director, so we had no problems. Mr. Shikata had used white powder and powdered his face completely white and was wearing a red blouse and grass skirt and did a hula dance while singing a Hawaiian song, and that made everyone laugh.

June 26

Today is a day off, I so slept till six. After breakfast, I did laundry. In the afternoon, I sewed Yoko's blouse again. Because it is hot, not much gets done.

Yoko was lamenting, "Mother, you were always saying when you turned forty-three, our luck was going to improve, and you were so looking forward to it, but there isn't one thing good with us."

It was misfortune after misfortune, and it is just as she says. But even with misfortune, if you hit bottom, things have to start improving—so I thought and consoled myself.

In Detroit and Los Angeles, a battle between whites and blacks took place, and it seems there were a number of deaths and injuries. They say in Detroit it started when a black male disgraced a white woman, but the one in Los Angeles started from an argument about the truth of broadcasts from Tokyo.

June 27

Mass layoffs to deprive inmates of spending money were being used as a policy to get people to leave camp. They say those who are left with jobs in various areas will have to work eight hours a day. In what world do they make people work for eight hours for 64¢ a day? We are not prisoners of war. If I am told to work eight hours a day, in the burning heat of the field, I will ruin my health, so I will quit.

In any event, the plan is to get even one person or half of a person out of camp. While labeling us as enemy nationals, this is so arbitrary. I wonder how Americans are being treated in Japan. We would like to know.

June 28

It was cloudy in the morning. When I went to the waiting area for farmers, we talked about workers in other fields having to work from eight to five from today. We half believed it as we went into the field. There we were told by our section Chief Mr. T that it was so. In any event, this is unbearable in one-hundred-thirty-degree heat in the sun where your feet get burning hot through the thick rubber soles.

That the government plans to reduce the expense of relocation centers by half and has ordered camp managers and officials to enforce mass layoffs and induce people to leave camp does not seem like its false. Everyone from section chiefs to all farmers are saying, "So getting two birds with one stone" and are angry and making noises. But they say anyone that goes on strike will be arrested. With this, farming became the hardest job.

July 6

By the fifteenth, as the first phase, it seems there will be a total reduction of three hundred fifty people from all areas. Even the mess hall, two who joined later were laid off. In my field around eight workers who haven't showed up for a while may be laid off.

They say America has problems on the home front. The first is, Congress passed the anti-strike legislation which had been vetoed by the president but overruled by Senate with over a two-third majority. The second is, going behind the president's anti-inflation policy in the budget of the commodity bureau, the subsidy for the supplement to the food bill was eliminated. The third is ignoring the president's opposition; the unification of the commodity bureau was accomplished by transferring the supplemental food fund. The sumo contest between the president and Congress is a bit interesting.

July 7

When I went into the field, we had scattered rain. In the rain, we picked tomato. The furrows having been irrigated, it was like wading in the field, and our shoes and trousers were all muddied up. Our shirt sleeves, chest, and back are green from the tomato leaves and stems. I felt sorry for myself in this miserable dirtied-up appearance. When I was a child, I was doing mischief and dirtied my clothes and was scolded by my mother, but that didn't compare to my present dirtied-up pitiful condition.

Experienced women farm workers are sadly muttering as they look at themselves, "We've turned very green. Once you get tomato juice on your clothes, it won't come off even with washing."

Turn green, turn green, to the core of the soul. This blue, this green, it is the color of hope.

I gallantly stuck my hands into the thickly growing tomato vines and picked the bountiful light red tomatoes. My basket was soon full. I empty it into a large basket. In Japan, I had never seen so many tomatoes on a single vine. After all, the soil in America is rich. Instead of trimming it down to one vine or two vines, it is left to grow as many as it can, and the tomatoes just grow and grow, and one can only be amazed. I thought if an agriculture specialist saw this, he would be envious.

The sight of everyone's green appearance smeared in juice looked honorable as if they were wearing medals. I have become spirited. I can go anywhere all muddied up, dirtied up, smeared with vegetable juice. I can meet anyone.

The fact that I can go into a world full of women who want to put on appearances and wear good clothes, looking like this without feeling any emotions means I have acquired great courage. I can resolutely go to the administration office wearing farmer's clothing. I want to show those white folks who worry about the fold in their coats.

I was told by Mr. M, who was a musician camouflaged as a farmer, "Mrs. Aoki, no matter how dirty a farmer's attire you wear, you are the only one who still doesn't look like a farmer."

I asked if that meant I was a failure as a farmer. He answered, "I didn't mean that." In the minds of many, it seems my prior occupation is still stuck there.

July 9

From morning, it is dry and hot. During the morning, I picked tomatoes; in the afternoon, I picked melons and cucumbers. On our return, I received ten green melons and five honeydews. We each put it in a sack and boarded our transport truck. Then someone said today there was a policeman at the camp gate, and all gifts were going to be confiscated—so there were many who took what they had received back to the shack and put it away—but I decided if it is taken, it is taken and boarded the truck with my sack.

From the truck from another field ahead of us, watermelon, honeydew, corn, and things are thrown out, thrown out! Large watermelon smashed with gaping red mouths scattered around was a sight. I shoved my sack in the corner of the truck, took off my cloth-face protector, and sat in front of it. Breathing slowly, without moving an eyebrow, sitting calmly, I took off my large farmer's hat and fanned myself. Three American policemen, three Japanese policemen, one Japanese policeman hurriedly up and in a low voice said in Japanese to those who had their sacks in the open, "Hurry up and hide it!"

The American policemen came to look, but we moved our bodies to hide the cargo. However, Mrs. XX's honeydew was discovered, and all five of them were dropped underneath the truck. Mrs. XX had borrowed a bucket used for harvesting with number 66 printed on it to carry her honeydew. The men farmers knew that if they were discovered using field buckets, it could be pesky problems, so they did their best to hide theirs; but with honeydews in full view, there wasn't much they could do.

We were passed with an "okay!" Those who had escaped the tiger's mouth rejoiced.

July 10

Today it was digging burdock and bundling. I said digging, but the field has a deep plow, so it doesn't take strength since the burdock comes right out. It is as the word says, burdock pulling. I wonder if they harvest like this in Japan now. Or is it still done like we observed in our childhood, digging burdock and mountain yam when it was really hard, people would dig it out one at a time by hand. They are bundled in two locations, but tying is done in a special way, and I didn't know how, so I learned from a real farmer. They are not thick but splendid specimens about two feet long.

On our return, today again, there is an American policeman and a Japanese policeman. The American policeman is shouting, "Unload all vegetables!" However, today's gift was a bundle of ten burdocks. Everyone placed their bundle by their feet and did not unload any. The farmers have a right to be the first to eat the product of their labor before anyone else.

The police say, "They are the product grown on U.S. government land, using U.S. government equipment, using U.S. government fertilizer and water, so we will not let enemy nationals have their own way."

The funny thing here is Caucasians regard burdock as nondigestible or poison and will not eat it, and so although the burdock could be seen by everyone's feet, there was no order to unload it. We were given the "go ahead." After passing the inspection station, the farmers on the transport truck laughed out loud altogether and said things like, "Stupid jackass!" "I won't forget!"

July 21

A postcard came from my husband by express mail. The contents were—it has been announced that I and my three family members are included in the next exchange ship. We are included among a small number of people, so this is reliable. Prepare yourself with that in mind.

I will have to think about sewing clothes to wear on the ship.

July 27

Last night, I received a notice to report to the Social Welfare Office at ten, so I went. I was told by the receptionist, Ms. Obata, "We received a telegram from Washington. On this second exchange ship, you three are to be on it, so please be aware of that."

"Is it a sure thing?"

I was laughed at. "Until you are on board, no one is a sure thing."

The ship is the Swedish ship *Gripsholm,* departure to be by September 1. Ah, we have finally become among those who will go around the world and step on Japan's soil. In that case, I will quit farming at the end of this month.

July 30

Today I received a kind letter from Rev. Tamai Yoshitaka, the head missionary of the First Denver Buddhist Church.

"Finally, it seems you will be returning to Japan. If there is anything you need, please let me know. I will send it."

My husband in Santa Fe will probably ask, but I thought that would be too brazen, so I gratefully accepted only the deep consideration.

July 31

With today, I will be parting with farm work. Taking seeds from tomatoes, my clothes got thoroughly wet from the juice being squeezed out.

Mrs. Y who was very playful and working next to me said, "With this, you will probably end your life as a farmer. The only time in your life. As a remembrance, I will put a lot of it on you."

So saying, she intentionally put tomato juice not only on my sleeve but on my back and on my trouser. After we finished work, I gave my apron and arm protector which had been laundered in a clean stream to Mrs. M and Mrs. K. Even though they are no longer of use to me, if one does field work, you need many replacement aprons and arm protectors.

At the watch shack, I informed the one in charge of attendance that from Monday to remove my name. When our transport truck arrived, the farm women all shouted, "Sayonara! Sayonara!" After we boarded the truck, Mrs. K said, "If you have any spare time from packing, please come to see us." And my eyes got teary. When I said farewell to Mr. Y who was in charge, he said, "In that case." And as a farewell gift and just for me, he selected seven large honeydew melons.

In order not to be considered as insincere or impertinent because I was a writer, I had tried my best and had always taken humble, a self-deprecating attitude.

"So to the field, sayonara, and to the produce, sayonara."

I am far from being an accomplished farmer, but for eight months, in the mornings and in the evenings, the hundred people I worked with, I was able to be one of them and understand.

Under the open sky, the fully exposed mind and soul of people—there is so much that cannot be said with pens or words, so many surprises and admirable things, and at times leaving me frowning.

Me, ah me! This time for sure, finally I will be able to return home on the exchange ship!

The End

Printed: September 20, 1953
Published: September 30, 1953
Author: Yamamoto Asako
Publisher: Aoki Hisa
Printer: Shirahashi Print Shop, Tokyo, Japan

Biography of Author
Real Name of Author: Aoki Hisa
Born: Thirty-Third Year of Meiji, Yamagata City (July 1900)
Education: Yamagata Girls High School, Tokyo Girls Teachers School, Second Main Division, graduated Nippon University, Upper Teachers Department, Japanese/Chinese Literature Division.
Occupation: Teacher at Tokyo, Honolulu, Oakland, Los Angeles, Writer for *Kashu Mainichi* newspaper (California Daily News)

Other books:

1939. *Kokoro No Kage* (Collection of Essays, *Shadow of the Heart*)
Published in Tokyo, Japan, and also sold in the United States, 1939

1944. *Teia Maru No Hokoku* (*Report on the Teia Maru*)
Published in Tokyo, Japan.

1953. *Eba Aru Haku Do* (*White Road of Thorns*)
Published in Tokyo, Japan.

1956. *Kana Shimi Wa Umi No Kana Tani*
Published in Tokyo, Japan.

1960. *O Shaka Sama No Ashiato Wo Tazunete*
Published in Tokyo, Japan.

ACKNOWLEDGMENTS

I would like to thank Archie Miyamoto from the bottom of my heart for translating Mother's book. This book would have never come to life without the encouragement of Archie Miyamoto, who volunteered to translate my late mother's book written in Japanese and published in Japan in 1953.

Archie spent many hours, days, and months from his busy schedule to translate her book. He read my mother's two books about the camp life and exchange ship. He said that her two books should be translated and donated to the Japanese American Museum for the legacy of the Japanese American history. Archie served in the U.S. Military for twenty-nine years and retired as a lieutenant colonel. He went through primary school in the United States, then primary and secondary school in Japan, followed by university and graduate school in the United States, and although he had native fluency in English and Japanese, while in the military, he served as an infantry officer, paratrooper, and army aviator. While he had numerous overseas assignments, including combat tours in Korea and Vietnam, it was not until his final assignment before retirement that his linguistic proficiency was recognized and he served as the joint defense planning coordinator between U.S. Forces and the Japanese. He is proficient in Japanese and English translation. He has written articles for many publications, in newspapers and books, and has translated many personal friends' articles and written publications for his Lion's club.

According to Archie, he used five dictionaries (Japanese to English, English to Japanese, English dictionary, Japanese character dictionary, and Chinese character dictionary) because my mother was a literature expert. She loved to use the classic old Japanese Chinese Kanji, which had more depth to the meaning of each emotion. It made the words very difficult to translate directly into English. My mother's book was not translated into fluent American English in order to retain her Japanese identity.

I also want to thank Archie's lovely wife, Kay.

Thank you to my husband, Eddie, for keeping me calm and picking up the loose ends when I got all wired up about the book.

Mary Yoko Nakamura
Daughter of author

HISTORY OF THE AOKI FAMILY

I had two elder brothers (Frank Tokuhisa and Roy Kazuo) and one younger sister (Grace Naoko Sachiko). When my eldest brother, Frank, finished sixth grade grammar school and turned twelve years old and my brother, Roy, was ten years old in the fourth grade, my parents sent them to study in Japan. They were scheduled to return to California after finishing high school in Japan to attend college in the United States. That was how our family of six became separated when the war started on December 7, 1941.

First, about my father, he was a Buddhist reverend and also an educator of Japanese language. He was unreasonably strict to my sister and me. When he got upset with us, it was like a flash of lightning, and with a loud thunderous voice, he yelled at us, but he never raised his voice to his students. He would calmly lecture them and give extra homework for their bad behavior.

When the war started, the FBI came to take my father away to the prisoner-of-war camp, and we were separated for two years. When we saw him again, he had changed and was a totally different man. I guess he really missed us, and he was not as strict, and he realized how much he loved us.

My mother was an intelligent and compassionate person who loved life, and she was a maverick in her days. She never wore makeup. Her skin was like silk. She only put cold cream on when she went to bed and put vanishing cream on during the day. She was loved by all her students, her friends, and her many newspaper readers. She always helped people who came to see her for advice.

Her father was a professor at a university and also tutored many educators privately. He encouraged his five daughters to attend university and obtain the highest education that they could each achieve. Two of her elder sisters became professors. Mother and the sister above her were educators in literature, history, and language at the university. Her youngest sister became a home economics teacher. Mother had one brother. He passed away when he was an infant.

Mother enrolled into the University of Japan, Tokyo. In her days, it was only for men. She was one of three women accepted to the university at the time. The emperor of Japan presented a gold wristwatch to the top student each year. She became ill three days before the examination and missed three days of lecture from the professor. The test covered many parts of the professor's lecture. She came in second highest in score and did not get the emperor's gift. She was so sick after taking the test that after she got off the streetcar, she fainted by the telephone pole. She was carried home by people walking by.

I found out Mother wanted to pursue a career in politics and improve women's rights and freedom for a better life for the women in Japan. After her big disappointment, she asked her two elder sisters if they had a bachelor friend or colleague at their school who would be going to the United States within a year. Her second elder sister's classmate was my father and was being assigned to Hawaii Buddhist Church of America and was leaving within a year. Her sister arranged Father and Mother's meeting immediately. Within ten months, they were married and they went to Hawaii.

Mother loved excitement, horse races, Olympic sports competition, any type of competition, and also movies. Every chance she got, she attended these types of exciting events, reporting and writing about them in the *Kashu Mainichi* newspaper. When she was asked by the *Kashu Mainichi* to cover the Academy Awards' *Gone With the Wind* movie, I remember her long powder blue gray crepe dress with long sleeves, V-neck line, and rhinestone buckle belt; she looked just beautiful. Mother was five-foot-four-and-a-half inches tall and weighed a hundred five pounds. Most Asian women were five feet in that decade. When she was thirty-eight years old, she got pyorrhea gum disease and had all her teeth extracted overnight.

Her younger sister came to the United States in 1937 and married a widower. They had one son a year and a half after they were married. My uncle attended college in Chicago, and he spoke perfect English. My aunt was a wonderful gourmet cook. Mother couldn't sing or cook like my aunt or keep the house clean because she was not interested in doing things like that.

Grace and I did most of the cooking because Mother was so busy writing, teaching, attending meetings, lectures, and all of the social events she was invited to. My sister and I did all the housework, and since studying was our first priority, we did not have much time to play.

After being sent to Japan on the second exchange ship with our parents, Grace and I suffered more than we anticipated. It was like landing in hell for Grace and me—a nightmare we did not expect. We were not able to buy food and everyday necessities because of shortage. Father enrolled Grace and me into a girls' school, but our schoolmates were not kind to us because we were American. The school sent us to do farm work, like weeding and cleaning up around the farm.

Our house was bombed and it burned down in May 1945. To survive, we had to construct a shack made of corrugated tin sheets which we straightened by using our feet. The school was also bombed so we were unable to go back to school. We retrieved personal belongings and household items that we had buried in our bomb shelter in our yard.

The war ended in August 1945, and we were lucky to be alive; the six of us survived the air raid bombing in Tokyo. The will power to live was our primary goal, and we made it by praying and taking care of one another.

Soon American soldiers were in Tokyo and needed interpreters. Many jobs opened up for English-speaking people. My two brothers, seventeen and nineteen, went to get interpreter jobs. They both got jobs the day they went to apply. My sister and I were a little young, fourteen and sixteen, but since we needed food, clothing, and money, we both went to see if we could get hired as interpreters too. My sister was very mature for her age, and she was very smart, so she got the job as an interpreter at the post office. She told them she was sixteen and worked very hard. I got a job at the Military Post Exchange as a junior accounting clerk and interpreter.

Grace, at the age of fifteen, came back to America. Many family friends helped pay for her ship fare. She went to work for a doctor's family home as a mother's helper, taking care of two small children after school for a modest allowance. She shared the room with the two children for two years while attending high school. Upon graduation with honors from high school, she lacked financial resources to attend a university full time to become a doctor, so she worked part time at a Japanese consulate office and attended college for two years until she got married. She encouraged her younger daughter to become a doctor, and she fulfilled her dream.

I obtained a civil service job in Japan when I turned eighteen and worked for one year and three months until I saved enough money for ship fare. My eldest brother did the same, and we returned to the United States together. My other brother came back to the United States soon after my sister returned.

As soon as I returned, I worked during the day and went to evening adult education every night and completed high school and received a diploma in one year. I got married and went to night school, took accounting classes and got a job in a CPA's office.

After saving enough money, my husband and I bought a house and started a family. My two brothers were both drafted into the army soon after the Korean War broke out and served two years. Both brothers got married and worked for the U.S. government until they retired and passed away at sixty-eight and seventy years old.

Father passed away at sixty-eight years old. Mother had a stroke and was hospitalized, and the day she was going to be discharged, she had another stroke and passed away. She was sixty-three years old. Grace passed away at sixty years old.

Getting back to my mother's diary, she wrote her diary when Grace and I went to sleep at night. She wrote it all in Japanese shorthand, making two copies at once on a tracing paper with carbon paper and used a hard lead pencil. She left one set along with her treasured books with her good friend for safe keeping.

When Grace and I were at the camp school, Mother sewed two medium-size duffel bags for our clothing since our suitcases were old and broken. What we didn't know is that she sewed her copy of the diary papers into the sole of the duffel bags. We did not find this out until end of the war when we went back to America.

My mother wrote five books, and they all sold well in Japan. With the proceeds, Father and Mother traveled all over Europe and India and came to the United States to see all of us twice.

I am grateful to have had a mother like that.

Mary Yoko Nakamura

Hisa and Sisters, Tokyo, Japan, 1919
(Hisa front row right)

Hisa and her fellow educators, year 1925
(Hisa sit on front row center)

Hisa, Mother, 1922

Daughter Mary Yoko, 1959

Daughter Grace Sachiko, 1950

Aoki Family, San Pedro CA, 1953

CPSIA information can be obtained
at www.ICGtesting.com
Printed in the USA
FSOW01n1316290216
17511FS

9 781503 592131